ROOKIE COACHES
GYMNASTICS
GUIDE

American Coaching Effectiveness Program

in cooperation with the
United States Gymnastics Federation

Human Kinetics Publishers
Champaign, Illinois

Library of Congress Cataloging-in-Publication Date

Rookie coaches gymnastics guide / American Sport Education Program in
   cooperation with the United States Gymnastics Federation.
      p.   cm.
   ISBN 0-87322-390-X
    1. Gymnastics--Coaching --United States.   I. American Sport
Education Program. II. USA Gymnastics.
[GV461.7.R66 1997]
796.44--dc21   97-31119
                                        CIP

ISBN: 0-87322-390-X

As of January, 1993, the United States Gymnastics Federation became known as USA Gymnastics.

Developmental Editor: Ted Miller; **Gymnastics Consultant:** David Moskovitz, USGF Executive Editor and Coaching Development Coordinator; **Managing Editor:** Jan Colarusso Seeley; **Assistant Editors:** Julie Swadener and Moyra Knight; **Copyeditor:** Molly Bentsen; **Proofreader:** Tom Rice; **Production Director:** Ernie Noa; **Typesetter:** Ruby Zimmerman; **Text Design:** Keith Blomberg; **Text Layout:** Tara Welsch; **Cover Design:** Jack Davis; **Cover Photo:** Photo Concepts/John Kilroy; **Interior Art:** Tim Stiles, Tim Offenstein, Gretchen Walters; **Printer:** United Graphics

Printed in the United States of America   10 9 8 7 6 5

Human Kinetics
Web site: http://www.humankinetics.com/

United States: Human Kinetics, P.O. Box 5076, Champaign, IL 61825-5076
1-800-747-4457
e-mail: humank@hkusa.com

Canada: Human Kinetics, Box 24040, Windsor, ON N8Y 4Y9
1-800-465-7301 (in Canada only)
e-mail: humank@hkcanada.com

Europe: Human Kinetics, P.O. Box IW14, Leeds LS16 6TR, United Kingdom
(44) 1132 781708
e-mail: humank@hkeurope.com

Australia: Human Kinetics, 57A Price Avenue, Lower Mitcham, South Australia 5062
(088) 277 1555
e-mail: humank@hkaustralia.com

New Zealand: Human Kinetics, P.O. Box 105-231, Auckland 1
(09) 523 3462
e-mail: humank@hknewz.com

Contents

Welcome to Coaching!

The sport of gymnastics offers young athletes a great opportunity to develop physically, psychologically, and emotionally. A gymnastics coach can enhance that development; but it isn't easy.

The *Rookie Coaches Gymnastics Guide* will help you meet the challenges and experience the rewards of coaching young gymnasts. We wrote this practical resource specifically for you, the gymnastics coach who has little or no coaching experience or training. In this guide, you will learn how to successfully apply coaching principles in teaching developmental gymnastics skills to young athletes.

The American Sport Education Program (ASEP, formerly the American Coaching Effectiveness Program, or ACEP) and the United States Gymnastics Federation (USGF) combined efforts on this book to improve the sport experience for many thousands of gymnasts and their coaches—like you. The guide serves as a text for the ASEP Rookie Coaches Course, and is part of the USGF Professional Development Program.

Again, welcome to coaching. If we can help you meet the challenges of your role with information, materials, or courses, please contact us. Good coaching!

American Sport Education Program
United States Gymnastics Federation

UNIT 1

Who, Me . . . a Coach?

If you are like most new coaches, you were probably recruited from the ranks of concerned parents, gymnastics enthusiasts, physical education majors, or former athletes. And, like many rookie (and veteran) coaches, you probably have not had much formal instruction on how to coach. But when the call went out for people to work with a local gymnastics class or program, you volunteered because you like children and enjoy gymnastics, and perhaps because you want to be involved in a worthwhile sport activity.

I Want to Help, But . . .

Like many new gymnastics instructors, you may not know much about the sport you have agreed to coach or about how to work with young, inexperienced athletes. Relax, because this guide will help you learn the basics for teaching gymnastics skills successfully. In the coming pages you will find the answers to such common questions as these:

• What tools do I need in order to be a good coach?

1

- How can I best communicate with my gymnasts?
- How do I go about teaching gymnastics skills?
- What can I do to promote safety?
- What should I do when someone is injured?
- What are the basic skills and progressions for gymnastics?
- What progressions will improve my gymnasts' skills?

What Are My Responsibilities as a Coach?

A coach assumes the responsibility for doing everything possible to ensure that the youngsters in his or her class will have an enjoyable and safe experience while they learn gymnastics skills. If you ever doubt your approach, remember "fun and fundamentals" are most important.

Provide an Enjoyable Experience

Gymnastics should be fun. Even if little else is accomplished, make certain your gymnasts enjoy themselves. Take the fun out of gymnastics and you will take the kids out of gymnastics.

Children enter sport for a number of reasons (e.g., to meet and play with other children, to learn skills, and to develop physically), but their major objective is to have fun. Help them satisfy this goal by injecting humor and variety into your classes. Such an approach will increase your gymnasts' desire to participate in the future, which should be the biggest goal of youth sport. Unit 2 will help you learn how to satisfy your gymnasts' yearning for fun. And Unit 3 will describe how to communicate this perspective effectively to them.

Provide a Safe Experience

You are responsible for planning and teaching activities in such a way that the progression between activities minimizes risks (see Units 4 and 5). Further, you must ensure that the mats on which your class practices

and the apparatuses they use are free of hazards. Finally, you need to protect yourself from any legal liability that might arise from your involvement as a coach. Unit 5 will help you take the appropriate precautions.

Teach Basic Gymnastics Skills

In becoming a coach, one of the most important roles you will take on is that of an educator. You must teach your gymnasts the fundamental skills necessary for success in gymnastics activities. You will need to "go to school." If you do not know the basics of gymnastics now, you can begin by reading the second half of this manual; then refer to gymnastics skills books for additional information. But even if you know gymnastics from a gymnast's perspective, do you know how to *teach* it? This book will help you get started.

You will also find it easier to provide good educational experiences for your gymnasts if you plan your class sessions. Unit 4 provides some guidelines for effective planning of practices, and Unit 8 contains a step-by-step description of six practice sessions (marked by a purple strip on the edge of the pages).

Where Can I Get Help?

Well-established coaches in your area are an especially good source of help. So are local gymnastics teaching professionals, USGF State Directors, and local coaching administrators. They have all experienced the same emotions and concerns you are facing, and their advice can be invaluable as you work through your first few years of coaching.

You can get additional help by watching coaches in practice sessions and competition, attending workshops, reading gymnastics publications, and studying instructional videos. The following organizations will assist you in obtaining more gymnastics coaching information:

American Sport Education
  Program (ASEP)
P.O. Box 5076
Champaign, IL 61825-5076
(800) 747-5698

United States Gymnastics Federation
Department of Educational Services
  and Safety
Pan American Plaza, Suite 300
201 S. Capitol Ave.
Indianapolis, IN 46225
(317) 237-5050

Coaching gymnastics is a rewarding experience. Just as you want your gymnasts to be the best they can be, learn all you can about coaching so you can be the best gymnastics coach you can be.

UNIT 2

What Tools Do I Need to Coach?

COACH

TOOL BOX

Have you purchased the traditional coaching tools—things like a warm-up suit and notebook? They will help you coach, but to be a successful coach you will need five other tools that cannot be bought. These tools are available only through self-examination and hard work; they are easy to remember with the acronym COACH:

C—Comprehension

O—Outlook

A—Affection

C—Character

H—Humor

Comprehension

It is essential that you understand the basic skills and progressions of gymnastics. To assist your comprehension, the second half of this guide describes sample skills and progressions and suggests how to incorporate these skills into individual class sessions. In the gymnastics-specific section, you will also find a variety of drills to use in developing gymnastics skills (see the pages in Unit 8 with purple bands on the edges).

To improve your comprehension of gymnastics, take the following steps:

- Read Units 6, 7, and 8 of this book.
- Refer to other gymnastics coaching books.
- Contact any of the organizations listed on page 3.
- Talk with other, more experienced gymnastics coaches.
- Observe local college, high school, and club gymnastics classes.
- Attend a USGF Coaches Education Workshop.
- Participate in the USGF Professional Development Program.

In addition to having gymnastics knowledge, you must implement proper training and safety methods so your gymnasts can participate with minimal risk of injury. Even then, injuries will occur. And more often than not, you will be the first person responding to your gymnasts' injuries, so be sure you understand the basic emergency care procedures described in Unit 5.

Outlook

This coaching tool refers to your perspective and goals—what you are seeking as a coach. The most common coaching objectives are (a) to have fun, (b) to help gymnasts develop their physical, mental, and social skills, and (c) to win. Thus outlook involves the priorities you set, your planning, and your vision for the future.

Although standard gymnastics competition is not associated with the skills and activities that young athletes perform at this level, there are a variety of games and activities that are appropriate. The sample lessons in Unit 8 provide some good examples. If you choose to incorporate competitive activities in class sessions at this level, you need to evaluate your attitudes toward competition and winning. Are you coaching for the kids, or are you coaching kids for you?

To work successfully with children in a gymnastics setting, you must have your priorities in order. Just how do you rank the importance of fun, development, and winning?

Answer the following questions to examine your objectives.

Of which situation would you be most proud?

a. Knowing that each child enjoyed participating in gymnastics
b. Seeing that all the participants improved their gymnastics skills
c. Having one of your students win every skills contest

Which statement best reflects your thoughts about gymnastics?

a. If gymnastics is not fun, it's not worth it.

b. Everyone should learn something every day.

c. Gymnastics is not fun if you do not win.

How would you like your gymnasts to remember you?

a. As a coach whose class was fun to be in

b. As a coach who taught good fundamental gymnastics skills

c. As a coach who produced winning gymnasts

Which would you most like to hear a parent of a child in your class say?

a. Christopher really had a good time this session.

b. Katie learned some very important basic skills this session.

c. Jake is happy he won several contests this session.

Which would be the most rewarding moment of your class?

a. Having your gymnasts not want to stop even after class is over

b. Seeing one of your gymnasts finally master a difficult skill

c. Winning a competition in your gym

Look over your answers. If you most often selected "a" responses, then having fun is more important to you. A majority of "b" answers suggests that skill development is what attracts you to coaching. And if "c" was your most frequent response, winning is tops on your list of coaching priorities.

Most coaches say fun and development are most important, but when actually coaching, some coaches emphasize—indeed overemphasize—winning. You too will face situations that challenge you to keep winning in its proper perspective. During such moments you will have to choose between emphasizing your gymnasts' development and winning. If your priorities are in order, your gymnasts' well-being will take precedence over your desire to win every time.

Take the following actions to better define your outlook:

1. Determine your priorities for the session.

2. Prepare for situations that challenge your priorities.

3. Set goals for yourself and your gymnasts that are consistent with those priorities.

4. Plan how you and your gymnasts can best attain those goals.

5. Review your goals frequently to be sure that you are staying on track.

It is particularly important for coaches to give all young athletes opportunities to participate. Each youngster should have the chance to develop skills and have fun—even if it means sacrificing a few minutes of class time to adapt a skill or repeat a drill. It would be better to take the extra time and effort than risk losing an athlete's interest in gymnastics.

Remember that the challenge and joy of gymnastics are experienced through striving to achieve, not through achievement itself. Gymnasts who are not allowed to participate are denied the opportunity to strive to achieve. And herein lies the irony: A coach who allows all of her or his athletes to participate will—in the end—come out on top.

ASEP has a motto that will help you keep your outlook on the best interest of the kids in your class. It summarizes in four words all you need to remember when establishing your coaching priorities:

Athletes First, Winning Second

This motto recognizes that striving to win is an important, even vital, part of athletic participation. But it emphatically states that no efforts in striving to win should be made at the expense of gymnasts' well-being, development, and enjoyment.

Affection

This is another vital tool you will want to have in your coaching kit: a genuine concern for the young people you coach. Affection involves having a love for children, a desire to share with them your love and knowledge of gymnastics, and the patience and understanding that allows each individual participating with you to grow from her or his involvement in gymnastics.

Successful coaches have a real concern for the health and welfare of their gymnasts. They care that each child in the class has an enjoyable and successful experience. They have a strong desire to work with children and be involved in their growth. And they have the patience to work with those who are slower to learn or less capable of performing. If you have such qualities or are willing to work hard to develop them, then you have the affection necessary to coach young gymnasts.

There are many ways to demonstrate your affection and patience, including these:

- Make an effort to get to know each gymnast in your class.
- Speak to each gymnast by name.
- Treat each gymnast as an individual.
- Empathize with gymnasts trying to learn new and difficult skills.
- Treat gymnasts as you would like to be treated under similar circumstances.
- Control your emotions.
- Show your enthusiasm for being involved with your class.
- Keep an upbeat and positive tone in all of your communications.

Character

Youngsters learn in part by listening to what adults say. But they learn even more by watching the behavior of certain important individuals. As a coach, you are likely to be a significant figure in the lives of your gymnasts. Will you be a good role model?

Having good character means modeling appropriate behaviors for gymnastics and life. That means more than just saying the right thing. There is no place in coaching for the "Do as I say, not as I do" approach. Be in control before, during, and after all classes and meetings. And it's OK to admit that you are wrong. No one is perfect!

Consider the following steps in becoming a good role model:

- Take stock of your strengths and weaknesses.
- Build on your strengths.
- Set goals for yourself to improve upon those areas you would not like to see mimicked.
- If you slip up, apologize to your class and to yourself. You will do better next time.

Humor

Humor is often overlooked as a coaching tool. For our use it means having the ability to laugh at yourself and with your gymnasts during classes. Nothing helps balance the tone of a serious, skill-learning session like a chuckle or two. And a sense of humor puts in perspective the many mistakes your young gymnasts will make. Do not get upset over each performance mistake or respond negatively to erring gymnasts. Allow your gymnasts and yourself to enjoy the "ups," and don't dwell on the "downs."

Here are some tips for injecting humor into your classes:

- Make classes fun by including a variety of activities.

- Keep all gymnasts involved in progressions and drills.
- Consider laughter from your gymnasts a sign of enjoyment, not waning discipline.
- Avoid sarcasm and jokes directed at specific individuals.
- Smile!

Where Do You Stand?

To take stock of your "coaching tool kit," rank yourself on the three questions for each of the five coaching tools. Circle the number that best describes your present status on each item.

Not at all		Somewhat		Very much so
1	2	3	4	5

Comprehension

1. Could you explain the concept of gymnastics progressions to parents without studying for a long time?   1 2 3 4 5
2. Do you know how to organize and conduct safe gymnastics classes?   1 2 3 4 5
3. Do you know how to provide first aid for most common, minor gymnastics injuries?   1 2 3 4 5

Comprehension Score: _____

Outlook

4. Do you keep winning in its proper perspective when you coach?   1 2 3 4 5
5. Do you plan for every meeting, class, and training station?   1 2 3 4 5
6. Do you have a vision of what your gymnasts will be able to do by the end of the session?   1 2 3 4 5

Outlook Score: _____

Affection

7. Do you enjoy working with children?   1 2 3 4 5
8. Are you patient with youngsters learning new skills?   1 2 3 4 5

(Cont.)

Continued

Not at all		Somewhat		Very much so
1	2	3	4	5

9. Are you able to show your gymnasts that you care?   1 2 3 4 5

Affection Score: _____

Character

10. Are your words consistent with your behavior?   1 2 3 4 5
11. Are you a good model for your gymnasts?   1 2 3 4 5
12. Do you keep negative emotions under control before, during, and after classes?   1 2 3 4 5

Character Score: _____

Humor

13. Do you usually smile at your gymnasts?   1 2 3 4 5
14. Are your classes fun?   1 2 3 4 5
15. Are you able to laugh at your mistakes?   1 2 3 4 5

Humor Score: _____

If you scored 9 or less on any of the coaching tools, be sure to reread those sections of the unit carefully. And even if you scored 15 on each tool, don't be complacent. Keep learning! Then you will be well-equipped with the tools you need to coach young athletes.

UNIT 3

How Should I Communicate With My Gymnasts?

Now you know the tools needed to COACH: Comprehension, Outlook, Affection, Character, and Humor are essential for effective coaching. Without them, you'd have a difficult time getting started. But none of these tools will work if you don't know how to use them with your gymnasts—and that requires skillful communication.

This unit examines what communication is and how you can become a more effective communicator-coach.

What Is Involved in Communication?

Coaches often believe that communication only involves instructing gymnasts to do something, but verbal direction is only one part of the communication process. More than half of what is communicated is nonverbal. So remember when you are coaching, "Actions speak louder than words."

Communication in its simplest form involves two people: a sender and a receiver. The sender can transmit the message through words, through facial expression, and through body language. Once the message is sent, the receiver must try to determine the meaning of the message. A receiver who fails to attend or listen will miss part, if not all, of the message. The receiver's expression will often tell you whether and how the message was received.

How Can I Send More Effective Messages?

Young gymnasts often have little understanding of the skills and progressions for gymnastics and probably even less confidence in trying them. So they need accurate, understandable, and supportive messages to help them along. That is why your verbal and nonverbal messages are so important.

Verbal Messages

"Sticks and stones may break my bones, but words will never hurt me" is not true. Spoken words can have a strong and long-lasting effect. And coaches' words are particularly influential, because youngsters place great importance on what coaches say. Therefore, whether you are correcting a misbehavior, teaching a gymnast to perform a backward roll, or praising a gymnast for good effort,

- *be positive, but honest;*
- *state it clearly and simply;*
- *say it loud enough, and say it again; and*
- *be consistent.*

Be Positive, but Honest

Nothing turns people off like hearing someone nag all the time. Young gymnasts are

similarly discouraged by a coach who gripes constantly. The kids in your class need encouragement, because many of them probably doubt their ability to do many of the skills. So look for and tell your gymnasts what they do well.

On the other hand, kids know all too well when they have erred, and no cheerfully expressed cliché can undo their mistakes. If you fail to acknowledge your gymnasts' errors, they will think you are a phony.

A good way to handle situations in which you have identified and must correct improper technique is to serve your gymnasts a "compliment sandwich."

1. Point out what the gymnast did correctly.
2. Let the gymnast know what was incorrect in the performance and instruct her or him how to correct it.
3. Encourage the gymnast by reemphasizing what he or she did well.

State It Clearly and Simply

Positive and honest messages are good, but only if expressed directly and in words your gymnasts can understand. Beating around the bush is ineffective and inefficient. If you ramble, your gymnasts will miss the point of your message and probably lose interest. Here are some tips for saying things clearly:

- Organize your thoughts before speaking.
- Explain things thoroughly, but do not bore gymnasts with a long-winded speech.
- Use language your gymnasts can understand, but avoid trying to be "hip" by using their slang vocabulary.

Say It Loud Enough, and Say It Again

Talk to your class in a voice that all members can hear and interpret. A crisp, vigorous voice commands attention and respect; garbled and weak speech is tuned out. It is OK, in fact appropriate, to soften your voice when speaking to a gymnast about an individual problem. But most of the time your messages will be for all your gymnasts to hear, so make sure they can! A word of caution, however: Do not dominate the setting with a booming voice that distracts the gymnasts' attention while they perform.

Sometimes what you say, even if stated loud and clear, will not sink in the first time. This may be particularly true with young gymnasts hearing words they may not understand. To avoid boring repetition and yet still get your message across, say the same thing in a slightly different way. For instance, you might first say, "Keep your arms straight in a handstand." Soon afterward remind gymnasts to "Push down against the floor, hard, when in a handstand." The second form of the message may get through to anyone who missed it the first time around.

Send Consistent Messages

People often say things in ways that imply messages different from their words. For example, a touch of sarcasm added to the words "way to go" sends an entirely different message than the words themselves suggest. It is essential that you avoid sending such mixed messages. Keep the tone of your voice consistent with the words you use. Avoid saying something one day and contradicting it the next; your gymnasts will get confused.

Nonverbal Messages

Just as you should be consistent in the tone of voice and words you use, you should also keep your verbal and nonverbal messages consistent. An extreme example of failing to do this would be shaking your head, indicating disapproval, while at the same time telling a gymnast "nice try." Which is the gymnast to believe, your gesture or your words?

Messages can be sent nonverbally in a number of ways. Facial expressions and body language are just two of the more obvious forms of nonverbal signals that can help you when you coach.

Facial Expressions

The look on a person's face is the quickest clue to what she or he thinks or feels. Your gymnasts know this, so they will study your face, looking for any sign that will tell them more than the words you say. Don't try to fool them by putting on a happy or blank "mask." They will see through it, and you will lose credibility.

Stone-faced expressions are no help to kids who need cues as to how they are performing. They will just assume you are unhappy or disinterested. So don't be afraid to smile. A coach's smile can give a great boost to an unsure young athlete. Plus, a smile lets your gymnasts know that you are happy coaching them. But try not to overdo it, or your gymnasts will not be able to tell when you are genuinely pleased by something they have done or when you are just "putting on" a smiling face.

Body Language

How would your gymnasts think you felt if you came to class slouched over, with head down and shoulders slumped? Tired? Bored? Unhappy? How would they think you felt if you watched them during an entire class with your hands on your hips, your jaws clenched, and your face red? Upset with them? Disgusted at someone? Mad at a parent? Probably some or all of these things would enter your gymnasts' minds. That's why you should carry yourself in a pleasant, confident, and vigorous manner. Such a posture not only projects happiness with your coaching role but also provides a good example for the young gymnasts who may imitate your behavior.

Physical contact can also be a very important use of body language. A handshake, a pat on the back, an arm around the shoulder, or even a big hug are effective ways of showing approval, concern, affection, and joy to your gymnasts. Youngsters are espe-cially in need of this type of nonverbal message. Keep within the obvious moral and legal limits, but don't be reluctant to touch your athletes and send a message that says you really care.

How Can I Improve My Receiving Skills?

Now let's examine the other half of the communication process—receiving messages. Too often people are very good senders but very poor receivers of messages. As a coach of young gymnasts, you need to be able to fulfill both roles effectively.

The requirements for receiving messages are quite simple, but people seem to naturally enjoy hearing themselves talk more than listening to others. You can be a better receiver of your gymnasts' messages if you are willing to read about the keys to receiving messages and then make a strong effort to use them with your gymnasts. You will be surprised what you have been missing.

Attention!

First you must pay attention; you must want to hear what others have to communicate to you. That is not always easy when you're busy coaching and have many things competing for your attention. But in one-to-one or class meetings with gymnasts, you must really focus on what they are telling you, both verbally and nonverbally. Not only will such focused attention help you catch every word your gymnasts say, but you'll also notice your gymnasts' moods and physical states, and you will get an idea of their feelings toward you and other gymnasts in the class.

Listen CARE-FULLY

How we receive messages from others, perhaps more than anything else we do, demonstrates how much we care for the sender and what that person has to tell us. If you care little for your gymnasts or have little regard for what they have to say, it will show in how you attend and listen to them. Check yourself. Do you find your mind wandering to what you are going to do after class while one of your gymnasts is talking to you? Do you frequently have to ask your gymnasts, "What did you say?" If so, you need to work on your receiving mechanics of attending and listening. If you find that you are missing the messages your gymnasts send, perhaps the most critical question you should ask yourself is this: Do I care?

How Do I Put It All Together?

So far we have discussed separately the sending and receiving of messages. But we all know that senders and receivers switch roles several times during an interaction. One person initiates a communication by sending a message to another person, who then receives the message. The receiver then switches roles and becomes the sender by responding to the person who sent the initial message. These verbal and nonverbal responses are called feedback.

Your gymnasts will be looking to you for feedback all the time. They will want to know how you think they are performing,

what you think of their ideas, and whether their efforts please you. How you respond will strongly affect your gymnasts. So let's go over a few general types of feedback and examine their possible effects.

Providing Instructions

With young gymnasts, much of your feedback will involve answering questions about how to perform gymnastics skills. Your instructive responses to these questions should include both verbal and nonverbal instructional feedback. Here are some suggestions for giving instructional feedback:

- Keep verbal instructions simple and concise.
- Use demonstrations, photographs, videotape performances, and drawings to provide nonverbal instructional feedback.
- "Walk" gymnasts through a skill, or use a step-by-step demonstration.

Correcting Errors

When your gymnasts perform incorrectly, you need to provide informative feedback to correct the error—and the sooner the better. And when you do correct errors, keep in mind these two principles: Use negative criticism sparingly, and keep calm.

Use Negative Criticism Sparingly

Although you may need to punish gymnasts for horseplay or dangerous activities by scolding them or removing them from activities temporarily, avoid reprimanding gymnasts for performance errors. Scolding gymnasts for honest mistakes makes them afraid to even try. And nothing ruins a youngster's enjoyment of gymnastics more than a coach who harps on every miscue. So instead, correct your gymnasts by using the positive approach. They will enjoy performing more, and you will enjoy coaching more.

Keep Calm

Try not to fly off the handle when your gymnasts make mistakes. Remember, you are

Coaches, Be Positive!

Only a very small percentage of ASEP-trained coaches' behaviors are negative.

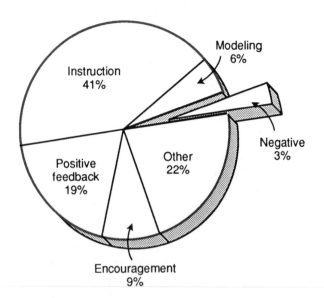

You can give positive feedback verbally and nonverbally. Telling a gymnast, especially in front of the whole class, that he or she has performed well is a great way to boost the confidence of a youngster. And a pat on the back or a handshake can be a very tangible way of communicating your recognition of a gymnast's performance.

Whom Else Do I Need to Communicate With?

Coaching involves not only sending and receiving messages and providing proper feedback to gymnasts, but also interacting with parents, other coaches, and facility administrators. So try the following suggestions for communicating effectively with these groups.

coaching young, inexperienced gymnasts, not elite competitors. You'll therefore see more incorrect than correct techniques, and you'll probably have more discipline problems than you expect. But throwing a tantrum over each error or misbehavior will only inhibit your gymnasts or suggest to them the wrong kind of behavior to emulate. So let your athletes know that mistakes are not the end of the world; stay cool!

Positive Feedback

Praising gymnasts when they have performed or behaved well is an effective way to get them to repeat (or try to repeat) that behavior in the future. And positive feedback for effort is an especially effective way to motivate youngsters to work on complex skills. So rather than shouting and providing negative feedback to a gymnast who has made a mistake, try offering gymnasts the compliment sandwich described on page 12.

Sometimes just the way you word feedback can make it more positive than negative. For example, instead of saying, "Don't make such a big kick into the handstand," you might say, "Kick your leg to vertical going into the handstand." Then your gymnasts will be focusing on what to do instead of what *not* to do.

Parents

A gymnast's parents need to be assured that their son or daughter is under the direction of a coach who is both knowledgeable about gymnastics and concerned about the youngster's well-being. You can put their worries to rest by holding a parent orientation meeting prior to the start of each session in which you describe your background and your approach to teaching gymnastics.

If parents voice a concern during the session, listen to them closely and try to offer positive responses. If you need to communicate with parents, catch them after a class, give them a phone call, or send a note through the mail. Messages sent to parents through children are too often lost, misinterpreted, or forgotten.

Remember, too, that parents ultimately decide whether or not their children participate in gymnastics at your gym, so it is necessary to do good public relations. Written updates on children's progress, monthly newsletters, and social gatherings are all helpful in promoting your program.

Other Coaches

Make an effort to visit regularly with other coaches in your facility and in the surrounding area. By developing relationships with

your fellow coaches, you create a support group should you have any difficulties with your athletes, parents, or program.

Other coaches are a good source of information. Sharing experiences with other coaches is a great opportunity to increase your knowledge.

Administrators

Whatever setting you work in, you are ultimately responsible to someone. Whether this person is a facility owner, program director, or school administrator, it is important to develop good rapport. This person may be your best source of information on the facility and program as well as support should any difficulty arise. Your relationship with the administrator at your facility is vital to the overall success of the program.

Summary Checklist

Now, check your coaching communication skills by answering "Yes" or "No" to the following questions.

	Yes	No
1. Are your verbal messages to your gymnasts positive and honest?	——	——
2. Do you speak loudly, clearly, and with vocabulary your gymnasts understand?	——	——
3. Do you remember to repeat instructions to your gymnasts, in case they did not understand you the first time?	——	——
4. Are your tone of voice and your nonverbal messages consistent with the words you use?	——	——
5. Do your facial expressions and body language express interest in and happiness with your coaching role?	——	——
6. Are you attentive to your gymnasts and able to pick up even their small verbal and nonverbal cues?	——	——
7. Do you really care about what your gymnasts say to you?	——	——
8. Do you instruct rather than criticize when your gymnasts make errors?	——	——
9. Are you usually positive when responding to things your gymnasts say and do?	——	——
10. Do you try to communicate in a cooperative and respectful manner with gymnasts' parents, other coaches, and administrators?	——	——

If you answered "No" to any of these questions, you may want to refer back to the section of the chapter where the topic was discussed. Now is the time to address communication problems, not when you are in the gym working with your gymnasts.

UNIT 4

How Do I Prepare My Gymnasts to Participate?

To coach gymnastics, you must understand its basic rules, skills, and specific teaching progressions of the individual skills. The second part of this guide provides the basic information you will need to comprehend the sport of gymnastics.

But all the gymnastics knowledge in the world will do you little good unless you present it effectively to your athletes. That is why this unit is so important. Here you will learn the steps to take in teaching gymnastics skills, as well as practical guidelines for planning your sessions and individual classes.

How Do I Teach Gymnastics Skills?

Many people believe that the only qualification needed to coach is to have participated in a sport. It is helpful to have been a gymnast, but there is much more to successful coaching. And even if you have not participated in gymnastics, you can still learn to coach successfully with this IDEA:

I —Introduce the skill.

D —Demonstrate the skill.

E —Explain the skill.

A —Attend to athletes practicing the skill.

Introduce the Skill

Gymnasts, especially young and inexperienced ones, need to know what skill they are learning and why. You should therefore take these three steps every time you introduce a skill to your gymnasts:

1. Get your gymnasts' attention.
2. Name the skill.
3. Explain the importance of the skill.

Get Your Gymnasts' Attention

Because youngsters are easily distracted, use some method to maintain their attention. Some coaches use interesting news items or stories. Others use jokes. And others simply project an enthusiasm that gets their gymnasts to listen. Whatever method you use, speak slightly above normal volume and look your gymnasts in the eye when you speak. Also, arrange the gymnasts so they are facing you and not another event or some source of distraction. Then ask if all can see you before you begin.

Name the Skill

Although you might mention other common names for the skill, decide which one you will use and stick with it. This will help to avoid confusion and enhance communication with your gymnasts. In gymnastics, a single skill may have several correct names or variations, so be sure to inform your gymnasts of these terms and how they are used.

Explain the Importance of the Skill

Although its importance may be apparent to you, your gymnasts may be less able to see how a skill will help them become better gymnasts. Offer them a reason for learning the skill and describe how it relates to more advanced skills.

The most difficult aspect of coaching is this: Coaches must learn to let athletes learn. Sport skills should be taught so they have meaning to the child, not just meaning to the coach.

Rainer Martens, ASEP Founder

Demonstrate the Skill

Demonstration is the most important part of teaching skills to young gymnasts who may have never done anything closely resembling the skill. They need a picture, not just words. They need to see how the skill is performed.

If you are unable to perform a skill correctly, have another coach or someone skilled in gymnastics perform the demonstration, or show a videotape performance of the skill. These tips will help make your demonstrations more effective:

- Use correct technique.
- Demonstrate the skill several times.
- Perform the skill slowly, if possible, during one or two performances so the gymnasts can see every movement involved in the skill.
- Demonstrate the skill on both the right and left sides.
- If necessary, break the skill down into smaller parts or learning sequences.

Explain the Skill

Gymnasts learn more effectively when they are given a brief explanation of the skill along with the demonstration. Use simple terms and, if possible, relate the skill to ones they've previously learned. Ask your gymnasts whether they understand your description. If someone looks confused, have him or her explain the skill back to you.

Complex skills often are better understood when they are explained in more manageable parts. For instance, if you wanted to teach your gymnasts how to perform a headstand to forward roll, you might take the following steps:

1. Show a correct performance of the entire skill, and explain its function as a progression in gymnastics.
2. Break down the skill and point out its components.
3. Have the gymnasts perform each of the component skills you have already taught them—hand/head balance in a tuck position, balance in a tripod, balance in a headstand, and forward roll.
4. After the gymnasts have demonstrated their ability to perform the parts of the skill in sequence, reexplain the entire skill and the safety tips that are appropriate.
5. Have gymnasts practice the skill.

Attend to Gymnasts Practicing the Skill

If the skill you selected was within your gymnasts' capabilities and you have done an effective job of introducing, demonstrating, and explaining it, your gymnasts should be ready to attempt the skill. Some gymnasts may need to be physically guided (spotted) through the movements during their first few attempts. Spotting unsure gymnasts through a skill will help them gain confidence to perform it on their own.

Your teaching duties do not end when all your gymnasts have demonstrated that they understand how to perform the skill. In fact, a significant part of your teaching will involve closely observing the trial and error of the performances of your gymnasts.

As you observe gymnasts' efforts in drills and activities, offer positive, corrective feedback in the form of the "compliment sandwich" described in Unit 3. If a gymnast performs the skill properly, acknowledge it and offer praise. Keep in mind that your feedback will have a great influence on your gymnasts' motivation and improve their performance.

Remember too that learners need individual instruction. So set aside time before, during, or after class to give such help.

What Planning Do I Need to Do?

Beginning coaches often make the mistake of showing up for their class with no particular plan in mind. They find that their classes are unorganized, their gymnasts are frustrated and inattentive, and the amount and quality of their instruction is limited. Planning is essential to successful teaching and coaching. And it does not begin on the way to the gym!

Presession Planning

Effective coaches begin planning well before the start of a session. You can take steps to make your classes more enjoyable, successful, and safe for you and your gymnasts:

- Familiarize yourself with the USGF, especially its philosophy, standards, and safety guidelines.

- Examine the availability of facilities, equipment, instructional aids, and other materials needed for classes.
- Make sure you have liability insurance to cover you when one of your gymnasts is hurt (see Unit 5).
- Establish your coaching priorities regarding having fun, developing skills, and winning.
- Meet with your superiors and other facility coaches to discuss the philosophy, goals, safety guidelines, and plans for the session.
- Ask gymnasts to provide you with a schedule of known absences or vacations.
- Institute an injury-prevention program if there isn't one in place already at your facility.
- Hold a parent orientation meeting to discuss your background, philosophy, goals, and instructional approach. Include a brief overview of facility rules and gymnastics terminology.
- Plan a meeting with parents for the conclusion of the session to report on the gymnasts' achievements, goals attained, and new goals for the future.

You may be surprised at the number of things you should do even before the first class. But if you address them well in advance of the start of the session, your classes will be much more enjoyable and productive for you and your gymnasts.

Class Planning

Activities during the session should reflect choices that will help your gymnasts develop physical, mental, and social skills and grow to love the sport of gymnastics. All of these goals are important, but we will focus on the basic skills and progressions of gymnastics to give you an idea of how to itemize your objectives.

Goal Setting

What you plan to do during each class must be reasonable for the maturity and skill level of your gymnasts. You should teach novice athletes the basic body positions and movements. Move on to specific progressions for more difficult skills only after gymnasts have mastered these basics.

Instructional goals for your initial classes might include the following:

- Gymnasts will be able to hold a variety of upright balance positions.
- Gymnasts will be able to demonstrate an inverted balance skill.
- Gymnasts will master proper falling and landing technique.
- Gymnasts will be able to perform three different leaps.
- Gymnasts will be able to execute jumps of 180° and 360°.
- Gymnasts will treat others with respect.
- Gymnasts will show concentration while attempting skills.
- Gymnasts will exhibit steady improvement in self-control.
- Gymnasts will demonstrate safety awareness for self and others.

Organizing

After you have defined the skills and progressions you want your gymnasts to learn during the session, you can plan how to use the consecutive class periods to teach them. But be flexible! If your gymnasts are having difficulty learning a specific skill, take some extra time to practice the skill—even if that means moving back your overall schedule. After all, if your gymnasts cannot perform the fundamental skills, they will not be able to execute the more difficult skills properly or safely.

But you do need a plan for each class. Six sample class plans are included in Unit 8 to show you how to organize your class and schedule specific periods of time for warm-up, instruction, and so forth. If this is your first coaching experience, you may want to use these plans with little variation. If you have some previous experience, you may want to use the samples as a model and create your own.

What Makes Up a Good Class?

A good instructional plan makes class preparation much easier. Have gymnasts work on the most basic skills and body positions in early class periods. And see to it that gymnasts master basic skills before you move on to more advanced ones.

Check all the equipment and mats that you will be using before each class. A mat that is torn or equipment that is not securely tightened creates a dangerous situation that may result in serious and even catastrophic injuries. Gymnasts should always wear proper attire—clothing that fits snugly without restricting movement and has no loose ends that could become entangled with the apparatus or the coach. Leotards, shorts, and T-shirts are all appropriate. Neither you nor your gymnasts should wear jewelry of any type.

It is helpful to establish one performance goal for each class, but try to include a variety of activities (objectives) related to that goal. For example, although your primary goal might be to master the fouetté, you should have gymnasts perform several different drills designed to enhance that single skill. Add more variety to your classes by varying the order of the activities.

In general, we recommend that you include these components in each of your classes:

- *Warm-up*
- *Practice previously taught skills*
- *Teach and practice new skills*
- *Cool-down*
- *Evaluate*

Warm up

Lead gymnasts through a 5- to 10-minute warm-up of mildly vigorous activities that will prepare them for participation, such as dance, jogging, jumping jacks, or skipping rope. Cold muscles are more susceptible to injuries, so avoid using extreme ranges of motion. Conclude the warm-up with specific stretching exercises for the skills being performed during the class period. See Unit 8 for a description of some basic warm-up stretches.

Practice Previously Taught Skills

Devote part of each class to working on skills the gymnasts have already learned. This is very important because repetition is a necessary part of mastering skills. But remember, kids like variety. So organize and

modify the learning environment to keep everyone involved and interested. Praise and encourage gymnasts when you notice improvement, and offer individual assistance to those who need help.

Teach and Practice New Skills

Build on your gymnasts' existing skills by providing something new to practice each class. Refer to Unit 8 for the proper method of teaching gymnastics skills. Use that section if you have questions about teaching new skills.

Cool Down

Conclude each class with a 5- to 10-minute period of conditioning and stretching. Muscle strength and endurance are the key components of conditioning, and repetitions of simple exercises like sit-ups and push-ups will help your gymnasts develop both. The cool-down lets gymnasts build their physical strength and increase their flexibility, both of which will improve their ability to perform gymnastics skills successfully. The cool-down will also help return the athletes' bodies to the resting state and avoid stiffness.

Evaluate

At the end of each class spend a few minutes with your gymnasts reviewing how well the class accomplished the goal you had set. Even if your evaluation is negative, show optimism for future classes and send gymnasts off on an upbeat note.

How Do I Put a Practice Together?

Simply knowing the five practice components is not enough. You must also be able to arrange those components into a logical progression and fit them into a time schedule. Now, using your instructional goals as a guide for selecting what skills to have your gymnasts work on, try to plan a gymnastics class you might conduct. The following example should help you get started.

Summary Checklist

Check your planning and teaching skills periodically. As you gain more coaching experience, you should be able to answer "Yes" to each of the following questions.

When you plan, do you remember to include

____ presession events like registration, liability protection, use of facilities, and parent orientation?

____ session goals like developing physical skills, developing mental skills, and providing enjoyment?

____ all class components?

When you teach a gymnastics skill, do you

____ arrange the gymnasts so all can see and hear?

____ introduce the skill clearly and explain its importance?

____ demonstrate the skill properly several times?

____ explain the skill simply and accurately?

____ attend closely to gymnasts practicing the skill?

____ offer corrective, positive feedback or praise after observing gymnasts perform the skill?

____ make sure gymnasts appreciate the safety tips for the skill?

Sample Class Plan

Performance Objective. Gymnast will be able to perform upright agility skills using the following body positions: squat, straddle stand, and straight.

Equipment—Station 1: tumbling mats; Station 2: floor height balance beam; Station 3: vaulting block

Component	Minutes	Activity
Warm up	10	Station 1: calisthenics, dance, stretching
Practice previously taught skills	10	Stations 1, 2, 3 (3 min each): body positions
Teach and practice new skills	25	Stations 1, 2, 3 (8 min each): Add agility movement to positions
Cool down and evaluate	10	Station 1: strength and flexibility exercises

UNIT 5

What About Safety?

A gymnast in your class is finishing up on the low bar at the uneven bars station. She seems to be in total control as she pushes away from the bar after a back pullover. She appears to have landed safely in the center of the mat, well away from the bar and the other gymnasts waiting in line. But suddenly you realize something is wrong. She has fallen, she is not getting up, and she seems to be in pain. What do you do?

One of the least pleasant aspects of coaching is seeing athletes get hurt. Fortunately, there are many preventive measures coaches can institute to reduce risk. But in spite of such efforts, injury remains a reality of sport participation. You must be prepared to provide first aid when an injury occurs and to protect yourself in the case of unjustified lawsuits. This unit will describe how you can

- create the safest possible environment for your gymnasts,
- provide emergency first aid to gymnasts when they get hurt, and
- protect yourself from injury liability.

How Do I Keep My Gymnasts From Getting Hurt?

The success of any gymnastics program centers on safety. And the most important factor in safety awareness is the training and education of gymnastics coaches and instructors.

Injuries may occur because of poor preventive measures. Part of your planning, described in Unit 4, should include steps that give your gymnasts the best possible chance for injury-free participation. These steps include the following:

- *Preparticipation physical examination*
- *Physical conditioning*
- *Proper apparel*
- *Facility and equipment inspection*
- *Warning of inherent risks*
- *Matching of gymnasts to proper skill levels*
- *Supervision and record keeping*
- *Warm-up and cool-down*

Preparticipation Physical Examination

Even in the absence of severe injury or ongoing illness, your athletes should have a physical examination every 2 years. Any gymnast with a known medical condition or pre-existing injury should have a physician's consent before being allowed to participate. You should also have each gymnast's parents sign a participation agreement form and a release form to allow their son or daughter to be treated in case of a medical emergency.

Physical Conditioning

Muscles, tendons, and ligaments unaccustomed to vigorous and extensive physical activity are prone to injury, so prepare your athletes to withstand the exertion of performing gymnastics. An effective conditioning program should include training for strength and power, flexibility, muscle endurance, and cardiorespiratory endurance.

ASEP Fact

In high school sports programs, gymnastics ranks fourth in the incidence of injury—behind football, wrestling, and softball.

Make conditioning drills and training programs fun. Be sure that you simulate the broadest categories of basic gymnastics skills. And don't forget, even the best-conditioned athletes need rest and water breaks. So make sure water is available to your gymnasts and that you give them time to catch their breath during each class.

Encourage your gymnasts to participate in a general conditioning program year-round. This type of program enhances gymnastics performance and also helps to develop an active, healthy lifestyle. The program should include but not be limited to aerobic training and balance, flexibility, and muscle strength and endurance activities.

Proper Apparel

Another way to minimize potential injury is to monitor the quality and fit of the clothes that your gymnasts wear. Clothing should allow freedom of movement, but not be so loose that it hinders safe performance. Proper apparel for girls includes leotard, shorts, and T-shirt. Boys should wear shorts or sweatpants and a T-shirt. Tights and pants may not be appropriate attire because of slick fabrics. There should also be no zippers on any clothing.

If a gymnast uses handgrips, a trained coach should inspect them regularly for wear and proper fit. Don't allow your gymnasts to wear jewelry of any kind, and remember that improper footwear can be dangerous. Also, make sure gymnasts tie back their hair so it doesn't pose a risk.

Facility and Equipment Inspection

Common sense and awareness are the watchwords for a safe and healthy environment. Remember to examine regularly the facilities, as well as the equipment, that your gymnasts use. Make sure that each piece of apparatus is in good condition, secure, and properly set up. Always check that your gymnastics mats are in good condition, adequate in number, and appropriate to the activity. Use gymnastics apparatus and mats only for the activities for which they are designed and manufactured. Always be alert for potentially dangerous conditions or situations, and report conditions you cannot remedy. Have your gymnasts participate in safety check inspections.

If there are any other activities in the gym at the same time as your class, check with your supervisor to arrange for some type of partition or organizational format to keep the activities separated. Your facility should also have a first aid kit, which you should check periodically and have restocked when

necessary. Post emergency telephone numbers by each telephone.

Warning of Inherent Risks

All athletic activities involve certain inherent risks, and gymnastics is no exception. Even under the best of conditions, injuries can and do occur, and because gymnastics involves inverted body positions, such as in somersaulting, the potential risks include serious, catastrophic injury and even death.

ASEP Fact

Catastrophic spine injuries have occurred from the improper execution of the somersault on trampolines and other equipment.

Make sure your gymnasts know, understand, and heed your warnings of the known risks of gymnastics participation. Repeat these warnings regularly and include safety tips in each lesson.

A presession parent orientation meeting is a good opportunity to explain the risks of gymnastics to parents and participants. A safety video is also available from the USGF

INFORMED CONSENT FORM

I hereby give my permission for _____ to participate in

_____ during the athletic season beginning in 199___. Further, I authorize the school to provide emergency treatment of an injury to or illness of my child if qualified medical personnel consider treatment necessary *and* perform the treatment. This authorization is granted only if I cannot be reached and a reasonable effort has been made to do so.

Date _____ Parent or guardian _____

Address _____ Phone ( )_____

Family physician _____ Phone ( )_____

Pre-existing medical conditions (e.g., allergies or chronic illnesses) _____

_____

Other(s) to also contact in case of emergency _____

Relationship to child _____ Phone ( )_____

My child and I are aware that participating in _____ is a potentially hazardous activity. I assume all risks associated with participation in this sport, including but not limited to falls, contact with other participants, the effects of the weather, traffic, and other reasonable risk conditions associated with the sport. All such risks to my child are known and understood by me.

I understand this informed consent form and agree to its conditions on behalf of my child.

Child's signature _____ Date _____

Parent's signature _____ Date _____

to assist you in presenting gymnastics-safety awareness to parents and athletes. It is also a good time to have both participants and their parents sign waivers releasing you from liability, should an injury occur. Such signed documents do not relieve you of responsibility for your gymnasts' well-being, but they are recommended by many lawyers, as they are proof parents and gymnasts have been warned.

Matching of Gymnasts to Proper Skill Levels

As a gymnastics instructor and coach you must understand that few young athletes can walk into a gym and within several weeks begin competing in gymnastics. Other sections of this book outline the need for proper skill progression. It is also your responsibility to evaluate and monitor the skill level of each athlete to make sure that the skills you are teaching match the gymnast's level of ability. Beginner gymnasts participate in recreational types of gymnastics activities, and as they progress in the sport they move through Junior Olympic or age group competition, sometimes high school and college competition; only a very few reach the elite level where they compete nationally and internationally.

You should evaluate each gymnast prior to participation to determine her or his individual level of skill proficiency. For safety reasons, it is critical that you teach each gymnast the skills and progressions appropriate to that level. By separating gymnasts into small groups and assigning appropriate tasks, you can keep the class moving and still do it safely.

Supervision and Record Keeping

With new or inexperienced gymnasts, your presence in the general training area is not enough; you must actively plan and direct training activities and closely observe and evaluate gymnasts' performances. You are responsible for their welfare. So if you notice a gymnast having any sort of physical or behavior problem, give him or her a break from participation while you evaluate the situation.

As a coach, you must also insure performer readiness, use proper skill progressions, prohibit horseplay, and check that the equipment is set up appropriately. These specific supervisory activities will make the participation environment safer for your gymnasts and will help protect you from liability in the event of an injury.

For further protection, keep records of your session plans, individual lesson plans, and gymnasts' injuries. Session and lesson plans come in handy when you need evidence that your gymnasts have been taught certain skills, and accurate, detailed accident report forms offer protection against unfounded lawsuits. Most clubs, YMCAs, and schools have sample forms that you can use or adapt. Complete them to the best of your ability and then hold onto them for several years so someone's "old gymnastics injury" does not come back to haunt you. Your insurance carrier may require that you file accident reports with them, also.

Warm-Up and Cool-Down

The warm-up and cool-down offer you a good opportunity to introduce skills and concepts, including social skills. Don't take the warm-up and cool-down for granted. They are vital parts of a successful coaching plan.

Although young bodies are generally very limber, they too can get tight from inactivity. A warm-up of 5 to 10 minutes before each practice session is strongly recommended. Warm-up should address each muscle group and get the heart rate elevated in preparation for strenuous activity. Easy aerobic activity (e.g., running or dancing) followed by stretching activities is a common sequence.

As your gymnastics class is winding down, slow gymnasts' heart rates with an easy jog or walk. Then spend about 5 minutes on stretching activities to help increase gymnasts' overall flexibility and avoid stiffness.

The sample practice plan in Unit 4 shows how to integrate the warm-up and cool-down. Unit 8 gives specific examples of exercises that are appropriate for warming up and stretching.

What if a Gymnast Gets Hurt?

No matter how good and thorough your prevention program, injuries will occur. And when an injury does strike, chances are you will be the adult closest at hand. The severity and nature of the injury will determine how actively involved you will be in treating it. But regardless of how seriously a gymnast is hurt, you must know what steps to take. Each gym should have written policies and procedures for dealing with injuries, which should include indentification of the problem, referral to a physician or specialist, rehabilitation, and record keeping.

Let's look at how you can provide basic emergency care to your injured gymnasts.

Minor Injuries

Although no injury seems minor to the person experiencing it, most injuries are neither life-threatening nor severe enough to restrict participation. When injuries occur, take an active role in their initial treatment.

Scrapes and Cuts

When a gymnast has a slow or moderate-bleeding open wound, follow these three steps:

1. Stop the bleeding by applying direct pressure with a clean dressing and elevating the injury, using gloves to protect yourself from direct contact with body fluids. Do not remove the dressing if it becomes blood-soaked. Instead, place an additional dressing on top of the one already in place. If bleeding continues, seek immediate medical attention.

2. Cleanse the wound thoroughly once the bleeding is controlled. A good rinsing with a forceful stream of water, and perhaps light cleaning with soap, will help prevent infection.

3. Protect the wound with sterile gauze or a bandage. If the gymnast continues to participate, apply protective padding over the injured area.

Sprains and Strains

The physical demands of gymnastics often result in injury to the muscles or tendons (strains) or the ligaments (sprains). When a gymnast suffers a minor strain or sprain, immediately apply the RICE method of injury care (explained on p. 30). If swelling, pain, or loss of function is evident after applying RICE, have the athlete checked by a medical professional.

ASEP Fact

The most common gymnastics injuries involve the lower leg and lower arm.

Bumps and Bruises

Inevitably, gymnasts make unplanned contact with apparatus and mats. If the force at impact is great enough, a bump or bruise will result. Many gymnasts continue to participate with such sore spots, but if the bump or bruise is large and painful, you should take appropriate action. Use the RICE formula for injury care, and monitor the injury. If swelling, discoloration, and pain have lessened by the subsequent lesson, the gymnast may resume participation with protective padding; if not, the gymnast should be examined by a physician.

Serious Injuries

Certain problems you cannot and should not try to treat yourself, include head, neck, and back injuries; fractures; and injuries that cause loss of consciousness. But you must plan what you will do if such an injury occurs. Develop an emergency plan of action that incorporates the following guidelines:

- Ensure the availability of nearby emergency care units and have a telephone and phone numbers on hand.

The RICE Method

R—Rest the area to avoid further damage and foster healing.

I —Ice the area to reduce swelling and pain.

C—Compress the area by securing an ice bag in place with an elastic wrap.

E—Elevate the injury above heart level to keep the blood from pooling in the area.

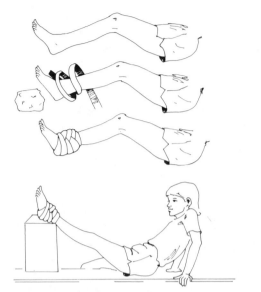

The RICE method applied to an ankle sprain.

- Assign another coach or nearby adult the responsibility of contacting emergency medical help upon your request.
- Do not move the injured athlete.
- Calm the injured athlete and keep others away.
- Evaluate whether the athlete's breathing is stopped or irregular; if necessary, clear the airway with your fingers.
- If breathing has stopped, administer artificial respiration. If the athlete's heart has stopped, have a trained person administer cardiopulmonary resuscitation (CPR).
- Remain with the athlete until medical personnel arrive.
- As soon as the first aid measures described have been completed, contact the gymnast's parents.

How Do I Protect Myself?

When a gymnast is injured, naturally your first concern is her or his well-being. Your feelings for children, after all, are what led you to decide to coach. Unfortunately, there is something else you must consider: Can you be held liable for the injury?

From a legal standpoint, a gymnastics coach has nine duties to fulfill. In this unit we discussed all but planning, which was covered in Unit 4.

1. Provide a safe environment.
2. Properly plan the activity.
3. Provide adequate and proper equipment.

4. Match or equate gymnasts to proper skill levels.

5. Supervise the activity closely.

6. Warn of inherent risks in gymnastics.

7. Evaluate gymnasts for injury or incapacity.

8. Know emergency procedures and basic first aid measures.

9. Keep adequate records.

After inadequate supervision, most legal problems for gymnastics coaches involve the concept of "failure to warn." This is an allegation by the injured party that the coach or teacher did not warn the athlete of the risk of injury associated with participation in gymnastics. This underscores the importance of warning gymnasts regularly, in words that they understand, about the risks inherent in the skills they are performing.

In addition to fulfilling these nine legal duties, you should check your insurance coverage to make sure your present policy will protect and defend you in case of an injury liability lawsuit.

Safety Certification

The United States Gymnastics Federation offers safety certification courses throughout the country. To find out more about the safety program and the next course nearest to you, contact

United States Gymnastics Federation
Department of Educational Services and
  Safety
Pan American Plaza, Suite 300
201 S. Capitol Ave.
Indianapolis, IN 46225
Phone: (317) 237-5050
Fax: (317) 237-5069

Summary Self-Test

Now that you have read how to make your coaching experience safe for you and your gymnasts, test your knowledge of the material by answering these questions:

1. What are eight injury prevention measures you can institute to minimize the risk of injury to your gymnasts?

2. What is the three-step emergency care procedure for scrapes and cuts?

3. What method of treatment is best for minor sprains and strains?

4. What steps should you take to respond to serious injuries?

5. What are the nine legal duties of a coach?

What Is Gymnastics All About?

 ymnastics is a wonderful combination of art and athletics, expressed in a variety of movement skills. Whereas other athletes use skills to move a bat, a racquet, or an opponent, gymnasts use skills to paint a moving picture—on a beam, around a bar, or with a ribbon across a mat.

Gymnastics is an activity that children engage in naturally during play. They love gymnastic movement, because it allows them to become their own roller coaster, with the body itself providing thrills as they execute each skill. This unit of the *Rookie Guide* will help you enrich young gymnasts' appreciation of the sport they love so much.

The Origin of Gymnastics

Gymnastics began in the early 1800s in Europe as a strict physical fitness discipline. The man credited most often with this start was German educator Frederick Jahn. Gymnastics was used as the basis of the very first physical education classes and later as a competitive sport to exhibit strength, balance, speed, and agility. Participation in gymnastics clubs and associations increased around the turn of the century, when hard physical labor was still a part of everyday life. The rigorous lifestyle made individuals well-suited to the physical demands of gymnastics. Around 1950 there was a marked shift from individual to team sports, with an emphasis on crowds of spectators. This lead to a change in competitive gymnastics from mass participation to smaller, more specialized teams. During the 1970s the general fitness of school age children declined, which made safety an issue. This in turn led to a decline in gymnastics participation and instruction.

Gymnastics Today

Gymnastics is based on body movements that involve swinging, leaping, or vaulting on large pieces of apparatus or tossing and catching various hand apparatuses. The heavy apparatuses used include pommel horse, parallel bars, and balance beam. Hand apparatuses include ropes, hoops, balls, clubs, and ribbons. The three major gymnastics disciplines are men's and women's artistic gymnastics and rhythmic gymnastics. Another gymnastics discipline, general gymnastics, still includes larger scale group activities and performances.

The range of gymnastics movements is very broad: walking, running, jumping, hopping, hanging or being supported by the hands and arms, rolling, diving, somersaulting, spinning. A gymnast may swing from apparatus, climb above it, vault over it, or rotate around it.

ASEP Fact

Some gymnastics clubs have as many as 1,500 students participating in their programs.

Apparatuses for the Three Major Gymnastics Disciplines

Women's artistic gymnastics—

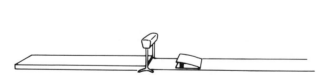

Side horse vault

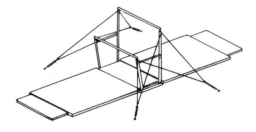

Uneven parallel bars

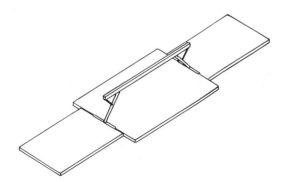

Balance beam

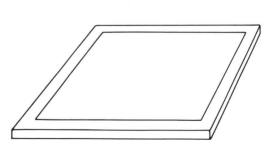

Floor exercise

Men's artistic gymnastics—

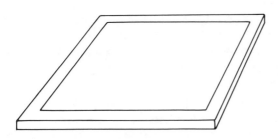

Floor exercise

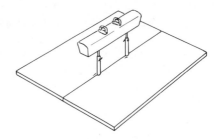

Pommel horse

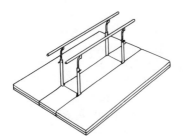

Still rings

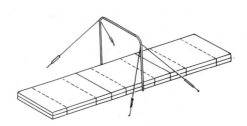

Long horse vault

Parallel bars

Horizontal bar

Rhythmic gymnastics—

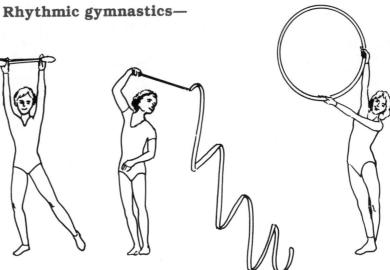

Rope

Ball

Clubs

Ribbon

Hoop

The events in each discipline for both men and women have many common elements. For example, floor exercise involves tumbling, balancing, rolling, and dance movements. Rhythmic gymnasts may dance and perform skills similar to those in men's and women's floor exercise, although they are not allowed to actually somersault. The rhythmic gymnast performs with various apparatuses—rope, hoop, ball, club, and ribbon—and leaps and jumps while tossing and catching each apparatus. Vaulting for both men and women requires a high-speed run followed by a jump and flight over a horse. The uneven bars for the women and horizontal bar for the men are similar in their large swinging and support movements. During the flight phase of gymnastics skills, the gymnast can perform many different types of turns, somersaults, and body positions before making a controlled landing or regrasping the apparatus.

Despite the commonalities, every gymnastics event has its uniqueness. Balance beam work involves many of the skills from floor exercise, but the gymnast performs on a beam 4 inches wide and 4 feet above the floor. Parallel bars and still rings involve swinging, somersaulting, and still positions that demand catlike agility and controlled, explosive strength. The pommel horse, requiring swinging movements in a support position, is another unique men's event.

These three disciplines and their many events make gymnastics very exciting, but difficult to master. You might compare it to the decathlon or pentathlon in track and field. Each gymnast prepares for several quite distinct activities involving artistic or rhythmic gymnastic apparatuses, with preparation quite specific to the discipline and event despite the common movements.

Preparing for Gymnastics

Performance of most gymnastics activities requires a certain level of technical training. Unlike sports in which only a few individual skills must be learned, gymnastics has potentially thousands of skills to be mastered. Because of this, gymnasts should attempt only those skills appropriate for their stage of development, experience, and ability.

A novice basketball player performs roughly the same skills—shooting, dribbling, and passing—as a professional player. They differ, of course, in the quality and consistency of performance. But in gymnastics, a beginner attempts only beginner skills and tries to perform them perfectly; an advanced gymnast attempts advanced skills and tries to perform them perfectly. Remember this when you work with both beginner and advanced gymnasts.

A second major difference between gymnastics and most other physical activities is the relatively high levels of strength and flexibility required for even the most basic gymnastics skills. If a gymnastics student is overweight, weak, or stiff, you should adapt your instructional level to account for those limitations.

A final difference between gymnastics and other sports is that it's impossible to "play" or compete in gymnastics without a repertoire of skills and physical preparation. In most sports, participants can play or compete right away because prerequisite skills are minimal and rules can be modified according to developmental levels.

Such is not the case in gymnastics. Gymnasts must first learn to safely perform a series of skills or combinations of different skills. This ultimately leads to developing a competitive exercise or routine, but the gradual progression of skills and creation of sequences may take a long time.

Getting the Basics Across

The rest of this guide will provide you and other coaches the instructional information you need to prepare your young gymnasts for participation and competition. Specifically, you'll learn how to teach your gymnasts the skills utilized in the USGF recreational and competitive programs.

Your emphasis should be on helping them master the appropriate skills and leading them through the proper progressions. When they've mastered all the basics, your gymnasts will be ready to learn simple compulsory routines or skill sequences and soon be ready to enter local competitions. But as you work to develop your young gymnasts' skills, always remember—kids participate in gymnastics for fun.

Competition rules, skill values, difficulty, and composition considerations are not relevant concerns at this level. Fun, fundamentals, and fitness should be the primary goals. You can emphasize fun by creating a positive, forgiving atmosphere that encourages "good tries" more than perfect technical performances.

Remember, even though you may have seen a skill performed thousands of times, your gymnasts may be doing it for the first time. Be enthusiastic about your gymnasts' initial efforts. Encourage them to use sound fundamentals. And devote plenty of time and energy to teaching them the skills that form the foundation for more difficult ones.

Increased fitness is an important goal. Strength, flexibility, balance, and endurance are fitness components you should try to develop in your gymnasts, regardless of their ultimate athletic dreams. Even a young athlete who ultimately participates in another sport can be served tremendously by the strength, flexibility, balance, and skills learned in gymnastics.

UNIT 7

What Gymnastics Terms Should I Know?

Every sport has its own terminology and vocabulary. The body positions, skills, and terms defined in this unit will help you communicate effectively with your gymnasts and other coaches. By using these terms correctly, you will demonstrate knowledge of your sport and your professionalism as a coach. There are literally thousands of gymnastics skills and positions, so for safety and efficiency make sure that you use the correct terms. If you have difficulty pronouncing these terms, practice saying them aloud and using them in sentences the way you would in the gym.

Spatial Directions

The body can be divided vertically in two ways—from front to back and from right to left. See Figure 7.2 for an illustration of the terms used to refer to spatial direction. To avoid confusion, it is important to give specific spatial directions to your gymnasts. Even simple gymnastics skills can become quite complex, but giving the proper directional instructions helps keep them in perspective. For example, forward diagonal is midway between forward and sideward, and backward diagonal is midway between backward and sideward.

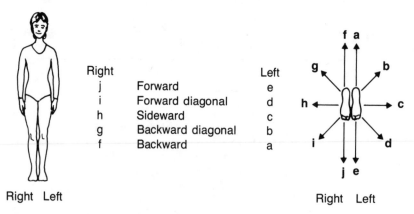

Right		Left
j	Forward	e
i	Forward diagonal	d
h	Sideward	c
g	Backward diagonal	b
f	Backward	a

Figure 7.2   Terms used to refer to spatial direction.

Levels: Positions of the arms and legs influence balance, skill performance, and aesthetics. Again, using specific directional terms will help clarify what you want from your gymnasts. Figures 7.3a and 7.3b illustrate the various levels of arm and leg positions.

a

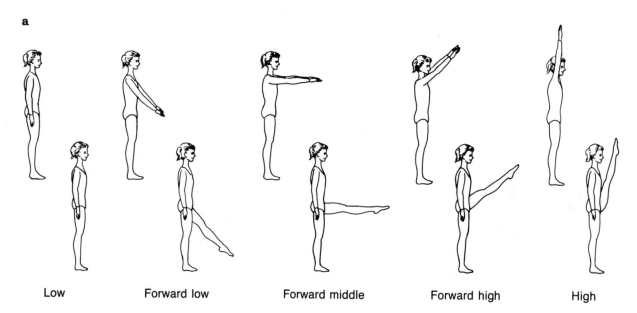

Low   Forward low   Forward middle   Forward high   High

Figure 7.3a   Specific directional terms to describe the various levels of arm and leg positions, viewed from the side.

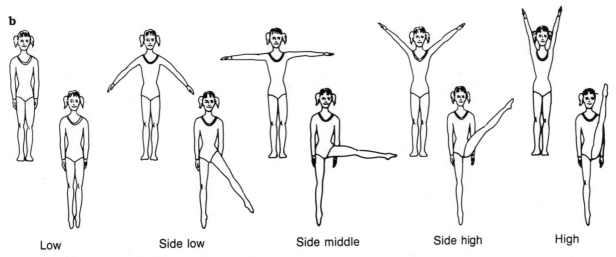

b

| Low | Side low | Side middle | Side high | High |

Figure 7.3b Specific directional terms to describe the various levels of arm and leg positions, viewed from the front.

Axes of Movement

Gymnastics skills involve rotating or moving along any of the three major axes of body movement—medial, longitudinal, and transverse—that pass through the gymnast's center of gravity. Remember that the closer the body mass is to an axis, the easier it is to rotate around it.

Medial axis: The axis from back to front (Figure 7.4). The cartwheel is a rotation around the medial axis.

Figure 7.4 Rotation around the medial axis.

Longitudinal axis: The axis from head to toe (Figure 7.5). A gymnast rotates around the longitudinal axis when performing a pirouette.

Figure 7.5 Rotation around the longitudinal axis.

Transverse axis: The axis from one side of the waist to the other (Figure 7.6). Forward and backward rolls are movements around the transverse axis.

Figure 7.6 Rotation around the transverse axis.

Body Planes

A body plane is an imaginary two-dimensional surface in which movements are performed. There are three planes, which correspond to the three dimensions of space. When a skill is described in terms of a plane, it means that the movement occurs in that plane. For example, you might instruct a gymnast, "Swing the hoop in the saggital plane on the right side of the body."

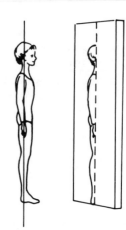

Frontal plane: Divides the body in half from front to back (Figure 7.7).

Figure 7.7 Division of the body along a frontal plane.

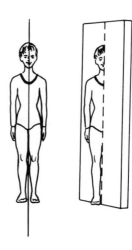

Sagittal plane: Divides the body in half from side to side (Figure 7.8).

Figure 7.8 Division of the body along a sagittal plane.

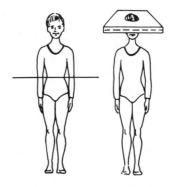

Horizontal plane: Divides the body at a given point, parallel to the ground (Figure 7.9).

Figure 7.9 Division of the body along a horizontal plane.

Body Positions

The following terms describe specific body positions gymnasts will use in performing skills. These are important terms that gymnasts need to learn in order to understand your explanations of skills and sequences.

Arch: The upper and lower portions of the back are stretched backward in a curve.

Hollow: The stomach and upper chest are rounded forward in a curve.

Inverted: Any position in which the lower body is above the upper body.

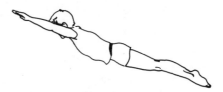

Layout: The body is straight and completely extended (Figure 7.10a).

Figure 7.10 (a) Layout;

Pike: The upper body is bent forward at the hips to an angle equal to or less than 90° while the legs remain straight (Figure 7.10b).

Figure 7.10 (b) Pike;

Prone: Lying face down with the body straight.

Straddle: The legs are extended sideways.

Splits: A movement of the legs, one forward and one backward, to an extended position at an angle of 180°.

Supine: Lying flat on the back with the body straight.

Tuck: The upper body is flexed at the hips and the knees are bent and pulled up towards the chest (Figure 7.10c).

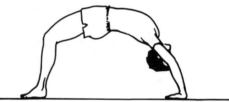

Figure 7.10   (c) Tuck.

Static Positions

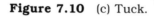

Static positions are specific body shapes that have no movement component. They can be starting or finishing positions, like the straight stand, or a specific skill performed during a routine, like an arabesque.

Straight stand: The heels are together, feet may be parallel or turned out (45°), legs straight, and torso and head erect, with arms at sides.

Bridge: An arched position with hands and feet flat on the floor and the abdomen raised (Figure 7.11).

Figure 7.11   Gymnast in the bridge position.

Arabesque (air-uh-BESK) *or* **scale:**   The body is supported on one leg with the other leg extended backward and chest held high. The arms may be extended in various positions.

Demi-plié (demi-plee-AY): A position of the legs and feet used in preparation for jumps and turns and in landings. The knees are slightly flexed and turned out along with the feet, and the head and chest remain upright.

Plié (plee-AY):   Any bending of the knees; feet remain flat on the floor, the body straight and upright.

Attitude (ah-tee-TEWD):   The support leg is straight while the other leg is turned out, bent 90°, and raised either forward or backward.

Support Positions

Many gymnastics skills involve being supported on the hands, requiring that the gymnast develop an upper body strength and balancing ability.

Front Support: Arms are straight and extended in front of the body (Figure 7.12).

Figure 7.12 Gymnast in a front support.

Rear Support: Arms are straight and extended behind the body (Figure 7.13).

Figure 7.13 Gymnast in a rear support.

Jumps

Jumps are aerial skills displaying momentary unsupported movements. The five basic jump distinctions are these:

Jump: Moving from both feet to land on both feet.

Hop: Moving from one foot to land on the same foot.

Leap: Moving from one foot to land on the other foot.

Assemblé (ah-sahm-BLAY): Moving from one foot to both feet.

Sissone (see-SON): Moving from both feet to land on one foot.

Six specific jumps are as follows:

Assemblé: The gymnast pushes up off one foot while swinging the other leg forward and up, bringing the feet together upon landing.

Cat leap, or pas de chat *(pah duh SHAH):*   The gymnast jumps forward off one leg while swinging the other leg forward and up, switches leg positions in midair, and lands on the take-off foot. The knees are bent 90° during flight.

Fouetté *(fweh-TAY):*   The gymnast pushes off one leg while kicking the other leg forward and up, executes a 180° turn, then lands on the first leg. The other leg remains extended back.

Hitchkick: The gymnast pushes up off one leg while swinging the other leg forward and up, switches leg positions in midair, and lands on the other foot.

Sissone: The gymnast steps forward on one foot, brings the other foot forward to a position behind the first, jumps and separates the legs to a split position, then lands on the first foot.

Stride leap: The gymnast pushes up and forward off one foot, travels forward, and lands on the other foot, showing flight (Figure 7.14).

Figure 7.14   Gymnast performing a stride leap.

Preparatory Movements

This category of skills comprises movements used to generate speed, power, or a specific position before executing another skill or series of skills. For safety and efficiency, you should make sure that your gymnasts can perform these skills correctly before moving on to more difficult ones.

Chassé (shah-SAY):   A springing type of movement (step-together). The gymnast steps forward with one leg and springs slightly off the floor, extending the legs to a straight position and closing them together. The gymnast lands on the back leg, with the front leg raised in preparation for the next skill (Figure 7.15). The chassé can be performed forward or sideways.

Figure 7.15   Gymnast performing a chassé.

Hurdle: A long, low, powerful skip step, which may be preceded by one or more running steps.

Lunge: A position with one leg bent approximately 90° and the other straight and extended back. The body is stretched and upright over the bent leg.

Inverted Skills

Inverted skills and body positions involve rotating the body so that the upper body is below the center of gravity. By following the proper progressions, you can teach your gymnasts to perform inverted skills safely and effectively.

Cartwheel: The rhythm of the cartwheel is performed to an even count of 1, 2, 3, 4 (hand, hand, foot, foot). The gymnast steps forward with one foot and lifts the other leg up and back while placing the hands on the mat in front of the support leg. As the body becomes inverted, the legs remain in a straddle, and the gymnast lands one foot at a time (Figure 7.16, p.48).

Handstand: Hands are flat on the floor shoulder width apart, legs are together, and the body is completely extended and in a vertical position.

Headstand: The gymnast places hands and forehead on the floor (head in front of hands) and extends the hips and legs straight up over the triangular base of support.

Figure 7.16 Gymnast performing a cartwheel.

Round-off: Beginning from a hurdle, the gymnast steps forward and pushes off one leg, swinging the legs up in a fast cartwheel-type motion. As the body is inverted, the gymnast brings the legs together while executing a 90° turn, pushes off the hands, and lands facing the starting direction.

Tripod: The gymnast places hands and forehead on the floor (head in front of hands) and extends the hips over the triangular base. The body is piked with the knees bent, resting on the elbows.

Hand Grip Positions

For support, hanging, and swinging positions, gymnasts must know proper hand grip and hand placement on the apparatus. If a gymnast's grip is incorrect, an accident or injury could result.

Overgrip: Grasping the bar with the thumbs pointing toward each other.

Undergrip: Grasping the bar with thumbs facing away from each other.

Mixed grip: Grasping the bar with one hand in overgrip and the other in undergrip.

Other Terms

Cast: The gymnast starts from a front support on uneven bars or horizontal bar, flexes at the hips (90°), then immediately thrusts the legs back and up while maintaining the support position with extended arms (Figure 7.17).

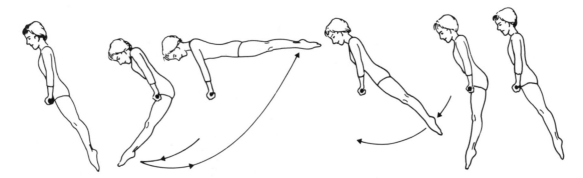

Figure 7.17   Gymnast performing a cast.

Chainé *(sheh-NAY):*   The gymnast executes a series of small, rapid half turns, usually moving on the ball of the foot.

Dismount: A controlled, upright landing performed at the end of a sequence of skills or a routine.

Flexibility: The range of motion through which a body part can move without pain.

Pirouette *(peer-oo-WET):*   A turn on one leg (Figure 7.18), a turn in a handstand position (Figure 7.19, p. 50), or a turn in the air while executing a jump.

Figure 7.18   Gymnast performing a pirouette on one leg.

Salto, or somersault: An aerial skill where the lower body rotates over the upper body. It can be performed forward, backward, or sideward.

Spot: To observe and physically guide or assist a gymnast for safety or when teaching a new skill.

Figure 7.19 Gymnast performing a pirouette in the handstand position.

Stick: To "stick" a landing means to execute it with correct technique and no movement of the feet.

UNIT 8

What Gymnastics Skills Should I Teach?

At first glance, gymnastics may seem extremely difficult to teach. There are thousands of skills across 15 events—is it feasible to know them all and have effective teaching plans for each skill? Perhaps not. But fortunately many gymnastics skills are so similar that you can easily progress gymnasts from one skill to the next.

Still, it helps to classify skills, breaking them down by events, activities, and skill families. Events are defined by the physical apparatus used by the gymnast and the skills employed while on the apparatus. Skill families are skills with similar movement characteristics: starting or ending positions, movement patterns, or directions of movement.

Teaching Gymnastics Skills

The skills and progressions described in this unit were adopted from two valuable texts—*Teaching Developmental Gymnastics* (O'Quinn, 1990) and *Sequential Gymnastics II* (Hacker et al., 1989). These texts are excellent resources to complement and extend what you learn from this *Rookie Coaches Guide.*

Developmental Gymnastics

Developmental gymnastics activities are designed for preschool children and appeal to their natural desire for play. These skills simulate all the major movement patterns corresponding to children's physical development. Teaching skills step by step is the safest and most fun for children because they build upon previous learning and experience success all along the way.

Teaching Developmental Gymnastics describes the proper sequencing of skills within each movement category for young or new gymnasts (see the categories following). This sequence provides a challenge that is just right for each maturational level. It will help you develop gymnasts' self-confidence, increase their sensory aware-ness, and, above all, allow them to learn skills that are safe.

Sequential Gymnastics

The sequential gymnastics program was originally developed for use by elementary physical education teachers. It includes skills and movement sequences that represent the primary movement categories but require minimal gymnastics equipment and spotting.

Sequential gymnastics is widely used by coaches and instructors in gymnastics clubs, community recreation programs, and school physical education programs. Its systematic approach to developing gymnastics skills is easily implemented in any program. *Sequential Gymnastics II* (third edition) is the skills textbook for the USGF Professional Development Program, Level I coaches accreditation.

The sequential gymnastics approach is very flexible and adaptive. It allows you to select skills from movement categories based on the availability of equipment, class size, athlete experience, curriculum goals, and so forth (see the categories following). You can also design the lessons to provide the gymnasts with opportunities for creativity, exploration, and fun.

Developmental Gymnastics

Station	Movement categories	
Mat/wedge table	Upright balance	Upright agility
	Falling and landing	Rolling over forward
	Inverted agility	Rolling over backward
	Inverted balance	
Vault/springboard	Forward bouncing	Rolling sequence
	Twisting	With table/over table
Low horizontal bar	Swinging under	Around the bar
	Support above bar	Rotating under the bar
	Grip change and turning	Hip casting
Balance beam	Balancing on level beam	Balancing on slanted beam
	Vaulting on level beam	Vaulting on slanted beam

Sequential Gymnastics

Station	Movement categories	
Mat	Upright balance	Rolling over forward
	Upright agility	Rolling over backward
	Forward wedge activities	Inverted balance
	Backward wedge activities	Inverted agility
Vaulting	Jump series	Flank and rear vaulting
	Front vaulting	Squat vaulting
Low horizontal bar	Circling backward	Swinging
	Circling forward	Support balance and
	Hip casting to sole circle	turning
Balance beam	Mounting	Nonlocomotor skills
	Locomotor activities	Tumbling
	Static balance	Dismounting
Hand apparatus	Rope	Ball
	Hoop	Ribbon

The Part-Whole Method

Because they are complex, gymnastics skills are best taught by the part-whole method. This means that when you teach a skill, you should break it down into smaller chunks, and then assemble those into the completed movement. For example, you can break a squat vault into many subskills: running, hurdling, jumping, flight to the hands, squatting motions, and landing. Once your gymnasts master these subskills, you teach them how to assemble the components.

You can teach one or more components of a skill during the same class period. But be aware that components vary in difficulty, and the more challenging ones will take more time for gymnasts to grasp. Also, assembling components is almost always more difficult than learning individual subskills.

Preparing a Lesson

Select skills for each lesson that will incorporate tasks in all four developmental domains: psychomotor, affective, cognitive, and social (PACS). Figure 8.1 shows the primary components within each domain. Coaches often focus solely on the physical benefits of sport, but young athletes are at a critical stage in learning cognitive and affective skills, attitudes, and ideals that they will use for the rest of their lives. Take the opportunity to enhance your gymnasts' skills in every developmental area.

The objectives of each lesson should emphasize all four developmental areas. You'll find it easier to create objectives for psychomotor development than for cognitive, affective, or social domains. Here is one way to incorporate cognitive and affective skills into your lesson plans: Add new skills and progressions, rotation patterns, or equipment configurations to create unique teaching and learning environments. By adding new skills, gymnasts can increase their gymnastics vocabulary and feel the achievement of accomplishing a new task.

Before you begin the skill part of each lesson, however, gymnasts will need to warm up. Organize the class to meet in a specific area of the gym for opening remarks; record attendance and describe the activities scheduled for the day. Ask if there are injuries or other factors that will affect anyone's ability to participate; deal with these, and then conduct a thorough warm-up.

Following the warm-up, have the gymnasts move to the first station, where you

Figure 8.1 Effective instruction includes developmental tasks from the psychomotor, affective, cognitive, and social domains.

will begin your instruction. *Sequential Gymnastics II* provides specific class organization schemes along with the specific skills and their events.

Organizing the Warm-Up

A big part of any successful classroom instruction—academics or gymnastics—is good organization. As the teacher, you must first decide what organizational scheme to use, then implement it effectively with your gymnasts. A highly structured setup may work the best with young and inexperienced students, and even for those with more experience for the first few classes.

Here are three organizational schemes—structured, circle formation, and random. You may choose one or use a combination for variety. In each scheme, the teacher (T)

directs the activities from a position where she or he can lead easily, observe, and supervise all activities.

For the structured scheme, the students are grouped in rows and columns facing you (Figure 8.2a) and perform the activities in place. The warm-up may be done on the floor or on mats. The circle formation is a very popular approach. Students move clockwise or counterclockwise at your direction (Figure 8.2b). The random scheme can be taught quite efficiently and safely (Figure 8.2c).

Timetable

Divide your gymnasts' warm-up time between these basic activities: aerobics, stretching, and preparation for the next activity (see bottom of p. 55).

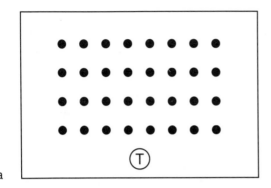

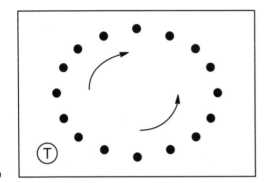

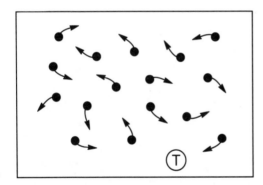

Figure 8.2 Three organizational warm-up schemes: (a) structured, (b) circle formation, (c) random.

Livening Up the Warm-Up

Using music or rhythm will enhance the warm-up and also add fun. Select music that appeals to the gymnasts and has a defined beat (in 4s or 8s, or an occasional waltz tempo).

If music is unavailable, you can count, clap, or use a rhythm instrument like a drum. You can also encourage your gymnasts to create their own rhythms by counting out loud, clapping, using rhythm instruments, or even doing chants or raps. You may prefer a very structured warm-up in which your gymnasts perform the same activities each practice. Or you might decide to use a warm-up routine that allows for some variety. Whatever warm-up you choose, make sure it fits your own teaching style and prepares your gymnasts for the activities that follow.

Warm-Up Stretches

Follow some easy aerobic activity with these stretches. Hold each stretch for 20 seconds, then release.

Side and Shoulder Stretches—Stand with one arm extended straight up, then tilt the upper body to the opposite side, reaching the hand up and across. Repeat the stretch on the other side. For the shoulder stretch, extend one arm across the chest, grasp the raised elbow with the other opposite hand, and pull the elbow backward. Repeat the stretch on the other side (Figure 8.3).

Warm-Up Timetable

Activity

	Class 1	Class 2	Class 3	Class 4
Organization and class instruction	1 min	1 min	1 min	1 min
Aerobics: start slow, then increase the activity/demand	3 min	5 min	6 min	9 min
Stretching activities: begin with large muscle groups, progress to small muscle groups; include coordination skills and games	1 min	2 min	3 min	4 min
Total warm-up period	5 min	8 min	10 min	15 min

Figure 8.3   The shoulder stretch.

Half Split Stretch—Lunge forward and bend the back leg to a kneeling position. Keeping chest and shoulders upright, press hips toward the floor. Repeat the stretch on the other side (Figure 8.4).

Figure 8.4   The half split stretch.

Modified Hurdle and Hip Stretch—Sit in a 90° straddle and bend one leg inward, positioning the heel against the opposite thigh. Bend at the waist and lower the torso toward the straight leg, and then toward the bent leg. Switch legs and repeat the stretch (Figure 8.5).

Figure 8.5   The modified hurdle and hip stretch.

Straddle Stretch—Sit in a 135° straddle and slowly stretch forward and to each side (Figure 8.6).

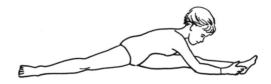

Figure 8.6   The straddle stretch.

Pike Stretch—Sit in a pike position; bend at the hips and slowly stretch forward, moving the hands down along the legs toward the feet.

Chin-to-Chest, Ear-to-Shoulder Stretch—Slowly lower the head forward, press the chin toward the chest, then raise the head. Then slowly lower the head to the side, press the ear toward the shoulder, and raise the head (Figure 8.7).

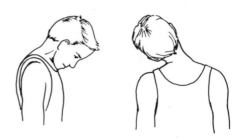

Figure 8.7   The chin-to-chest, ear-to-shoulder stretch.

Shoulder Balance, Tuck to Either Side Stretch—Lie supine, pull the knees to a tuck, and roll backward slowly to the base of the neck, keeping the knees together. Stretch the legs backward to one side of the head. Repeat the stretch to the other side.

Bent Knee Sit-Ups—Lie supine with knees bent 90° and feet flat on the floor. The hands should be placed across the chest or with fingertips touching the ears, not clasped behind the head. Beginning with the head, slowly curl the upper body forward. Stop before reaching a full sitting position, and slowly return to the floor (Figure 8.8).

Figure 8.8   Bent knee sit-ups.

Squat-Extend—Lie supine with knees bent 90^0 and thighs perpendicular to the floor. Curl the upper body forward while pulling the knees in to a tight tucked position; reverse that movement and finish with legs extended 6 inches above the floor.

Forward Shoulder Stretch—Using a ballet bar, low parallel bar, single rail, or low horizontal bar, stand with hands slightly beyond shoulder width apart. Bend slowly forward, allowing the shoulders to rotate inward and the chest to drop below the bar.

Rear Shoulder Stretch—Using a ballet bar, low parallel bar, single rail, or low horizontal bar, stand facing away from the bar. Grasp the bar with hands slightly beyond shoulder width and thumbs facing out. Slowly push the knees and hips out away from the bar. The body bows slightly (a bridge-like look). Allow the shoulders and the back to drop below the bar (Figure 8.9).

Wrist Press—Sitting or standing, place palms together, raise the elbows, push hands together, and hold. Repeat pushing the backs of the hands together; alternate several times.

Figure 8.9   The rear shoulder stretch.

Wrist Roll—Sitting or standing, place palms together, interlock the fingers, and rotate the wrists, making large circles around the hands. Perform the stretch in the opposite direction as well.

Sample Lessons

Six sample gymnastics lessons follow. Each lesson is designed to teach a variety of skills appropriate for beginner gymnasts. Use these lessons and the skill demonstrations that accompany them as models for your own instruction. If you are a new coach, you may decide to follow the lessons closely. As you begin to create your own lesson plans, modify and adapt the lessons in this unit to fit your own style.

Lesson #1: *Balance*

PACS SKILL OBJECTIVES

Psychomotor: To improve gymnast's static and dynamic balance.

Affective: To develop gymnast's respect for the work space of self and others.

Cognitive: To develop gymnast's concentration and cue recognition for repetitive sequenced motor skills.

Social: To develop gymnast's ability to attend to instruction.

TIMETABLE

Lesson 1 is ideal for a group of 30 to 35 gymnasts. This is a common size in school physical education classes and YMCA and recreation programs. The selected skills are relatively easy and require minimum spotting. The first lesson reduces the time gymnasts spend on individual apparatus to free up more time for group activities at the beginning and end of class.

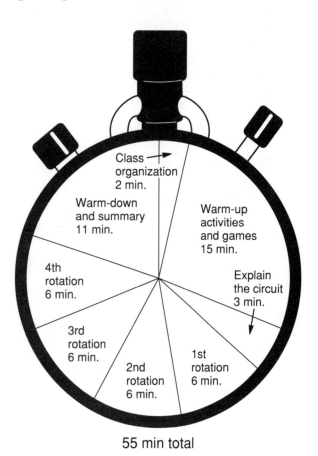

55 min total

FLOOR PLAN

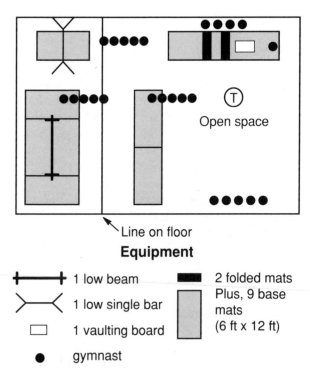

↖ Line on floor

Equipment

┣━━━━┫ 1 low beam	▬▬▬ 2 folded mats
╳╳ 1 low single bar	Plus, 9 base mats (6 ft x 12 ft)
▭ 1 vaulting board	
● gymnast	

Hand apparatus, balls, ropes, hoops, bean-bags, etc.

STATIONS

There are five stations in this circuit:

Mat and Open Areas—This is a combined station. The tumbling strip is two base mats positioned end to end.

Balance—Surround the low beam with base mats for safety.

Single Bar—Position the bar at chest height of the average-size student over a base mat or skill cushion.

Vault—Position two base mats end to end. Place two folded panel mats crossways on the base mats, slightly separated. Position the vaulting board close to one of the panel mats.

Jump Rope—This can be performed in any open space, such as the warm-up area. You needn't lay down mats, but it is a good idea to have gymnasts jump on a carpeted surface, which provides more cushioning.

BALANCE SKILLS

MAT

Upright Balance

V-sit: Sitting on the mat, gymnast slides feet toward buttocks (to the tuck position), with hands on the mat next to hips. To complete the V-sit, the gymnast lifts and extends legs to a V position, then takes hands off the mat.

Lunge: Gymnast steps forward to stand in the lunge position (with the knee of the front leg flexed) and holds.

Arabesque scale: The gymnast begins standing on both feet, keeping the upper body vertical and extended, then lifts one leg backward while maintaining a vertical curve. For the scale, the gymnast lowers the upper body while raising and holding the back leg.

VAULT

Jump Series

Rebound, jump, jump, tuck, jump: The gymnast runs forward, rebounds off the springboard to the first mat, jumps to the second mat, tuck jumps off the second mat, and lands in a demi-plié (Figure 8.10).

Rebound, jump, jump, straddle jump: The gymnast runs forward, rebounds off the springboard to the first mat, then rebounds in a continuous series, finishing with a straddle jump off the second mat and landing in a demi-plié.

Rebound, jump, jump, pike jump: The gymnast runs forward, rebounds off the springboard to the first mat, then rebounds in a continuous series to a pike jump landing, and lands in a demi-plié.

Lesson #1

TEACHING TIPS

Lesson 1 works best with beginner gymnasts; although they do get to try out the equipment, most of the activities take place on the floor. The group activities provide a good opportunity to use movement and gymnastics games.

When you explain the progression of activities, draw a picture of the circuit and explain the skills to be performed at each station. Your gymnasts can use the drawing as a reminder as they progress from station to station.

Figure 8.10 Gymnast performing the rebound, jump, jump, tuck jump vaulting series.

BALANCE

Locomotor Activities

Walk forward and backward: The gymnast stands on one end of a low or floor-level beam and walks forward and then backward.

Dip steps forward and backward: The gymnast walks forward, flexing one knee, "dipping" the other foot down the side of the beam with each step, and then bringing the foot up and placing it in front of the support foot. The gymnast reverses the process when walking backward.

Slide steps sideward: Standing sideways on the beam, the gymnast slides one foot to the side and closes the other foot to it, moving to one side, then the other.

BAR

Swinging

Run through, 180° turn, stop, run through: From a standing position with extended arms and overgrip, the gymnast runs under the bar, stops, releases the bar, turns 180°, regrips, and then runs through again.

Run through, 180° turn, stop, swing through (tuck): The gymnast stands with extended arms and overgrip, runs under the bar, stops, releases the bar, turns 180°, regrips, and swings under in the tuck position.

Swing through (tuck), 180° turn, stop, swing through (tuck): The gymnast stands with extended arms and overgrip, then swings under the bar in the tuck position, stops, releases the bar, turns 180°, regrips, swings under the bar in the tuck position, and stops.

JUMP ROPE

Forward Circle Series

Saggital circles, counterclockwise: Holding one end of the rope in each hand, the gymnast circles the rope 5 times counterclockwise on the right side of the body.

Saggital circles, clockwise: The gymnast circles the rope 5 times clockwise on the left side of the body.

Figure 8: Building on the previous two skills, the student alternates counterclockwise and clockwise saggital circles, first to the right, then to the left.

(Repeat each skill as needed.)

Jumping Series

Forward jump: Holding one end of the rope in each hand, the gymnast turns the rope forward and jumps 10 times in a tight springing motion.

Backward jump: The athlete turns the rope backward and jumps 10 times with a rebound.

(Repeat each skill as needed.)

Lesson #2: *Moving Backward*

PACS SKILL OBJECTIVES

Psychomotor: To improve gymnast's spatial orientation while moving backward.

Affective: To build gymnast's sense of accomplishment for new or different activities.

Cognitive: To help gymnast visualize backward movement patterns.

Social: To encourage respect for other gymnasts' efforts to concentrate.

TIMETABLE

Lesson 2 works well for a group of 30 to 35 gymnasts. This is a common size in school physical education classes and YMCA and recreation programs.

FLOOR PLAN

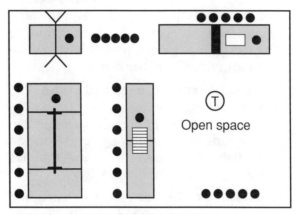

Equipment

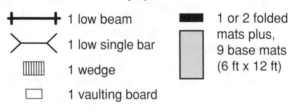

┼───────┼	1 low beam
✕─────✕	1 low single bar
▓▓▓▓▓	1 wedge
▭	1 vaulting board
●	gymnast

1 or 2 folded mats plus, 9 base mats (6 ft x 12 ft)

Hand apparatus, balls, ropes, hoops, bean-bags, etc.

STATIONS

There are five stations in this circuit:

Single Bar—Position the bar about chest high over a base mat or skill cushion.

Vault—Position two base mats end to end and center a vault on the mats. (For the vault, use a low horse, a mat shape [e.g., a trapezoid], a vaulting "box," or stacked bifold mats.) A vaulting board is also required. You may decide to use a landing mat or skill cushion on the afterflight side of the vault.

Jump Rope—Gymnasts may perform these skills in any open space, with or without mats.

Mat—Position two base mats end to end, and center a wedge mat on the mats.

Balance—Use a low beam (4 to 12 inches high); surround with base mats for safety.

50 min total

MOVING BACKWARD SKILLS

MAT
Backward Wedge Rolling

Roll back to jump, 180° turn, stand, forward roll: The student sits on the high edge of the wedge, rolls backward, and as the feet gain support, jumps with a 180° turn and does a forward roll.

Back roll straddle, back roll stand: The gymnast sits on the high edge of the wedge and performs a straddle roll backward; in completing the roll the gymnast does a tuck back roll on the mat and finishes standing in a stretched position.

Back roll extension: This activity should be done with a spotter. The gymnast sits on the high edge of the wedge and rolls backward, placing hands on the wedge by the shoulders. The gymnast extends at the hips and knees as the body becomes inverted, pushing the arms to raise the body. Stepping down one leg at a time, the gymnast finishes in a lunge (Figure 8.11).

VAULT
Flank and Rear Vaulting

Bounce and push with arms, 180° turn to seated position: The gymnast rebounds off the board, places hands on top of the mats and pushes with weight on the hands, then turns 180° to a seated position on the mats.

Vault to piked sitting position: The gymnast rebounds off the board, pushes off the mats with both hands, then pikes and turns sideways to a seated position on top of the mats.

Rear vault: The gymnast runs and rebounds off the board, pushes off with hands, then pikes and turns sideways, passing over the top of the mats and landing in a standing position with the side of the body toward the mats.

TEACHING TIPS

This is an ambitious lesson plan, but the selected skills are very easy. To allow more time for explanation and participation, you could reduce the number of stations, reduce the number of skills at each station, or set up all equipment before the lesson.

BALANCE
Nonlocomotor Activities

Arabesque 180° turn: The gymnast faces the end of the beam with one foot in front of the other, lifts the back leg to a low arabesque, raises up onto the ball of the foot, and performs a 180° turn (pivot) to

Figure 8.11 Gymnast performing a back roll extension toward a handstand.

face the opposite end of the beam, with arabesque leg finishing in front, low.

Forward swing turn: The gymnast faces the end of the beam with one foot in front of the other, swings the back leg forward and up, raises onto the toe of the support leg, and turns 180°, lowering the leg to the beam and finishing in a lunge.

Backward swing turn: The gymnast faces the end of the beam with one foot in front of the other, swings the front leg backward and up, raises onto the toe of the support leg, and turns 180°, lowering the leg to the beam.

BAR
Circling Backward

Back hip pullover: From a stand, with hands in overgrip, the gymnast jumps up and forward, pulling the bar toward the waist, then immediately lifts the legs forward and up and rotates the upper body backward, circling the bar to finish in a front support.

Front support cast: From a front support position with hands in overgrip and hips flexed with shoulders slightly forward, the gymnast thrusts the legs backward and up (hip extension), extends the body to a straight horizontal position, and lowers slowly back to front support before flexing at the hips.

Cast, back hip circle: This activity should be done with a spotter. From a front support position with hands in overgrip, the athlete casts and rocks backward holding the bar firmly at the hips, rotates around the bar, and finishes in front support.

SAFETY TIPS

The back roll extension on the wedge and the cast back hip circle on the bar both require spotting. Unless you have an assistant, restrict all activities requiring spotting to a single station.

JUMP ROPE
Forward Circle Series

Saggital circles, counterclockwise: The gymnast circles the rope 5 times counterclockwise on the right side of the body.

Saggital circles, clockwise: The gymnast circles the rope 5 times clockwise on the left side of the body.

Figure 8: The gymnast alternates the counterclockwise and clockwise saggital circles, first to the right, then to the left.

(Skills are performed with both ends of the rope in the right hand, then repeated using the left hand.)

Jumping Series

Forward jump: Holding one end of the rope in each hand, the student turns the rope forward and jumps 10 times with a rebound.

Backward jump: The gymnast turns the rope backward and jumps 10 times with a rebound.

(Jumps should be performed with rhythm, so music is recommended.)

Lesson #3: *Strength*

PACS SKILL OBJECTIVES

Psychomotor: To improve gymnast's strength development, particularly in the upper body.

Affective: To develop gymnast's sense of achievement for new or different skills.

Cognitive: To broaden gymnast's vocabulary, including skill and apparatus terminology.

Social: To foster gymnast's cooperation with other athletes.

TIMETABLE

Lesson 3 is designed for a class of 25 to 30 athletes and uses a time frame that often occurs in school physical education programs.

FLOOR PLAN

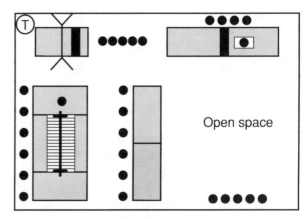

Equipment

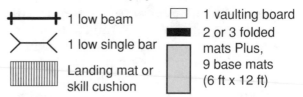

┼━┼ 1 low beam	☐ 1 vaulting board
✕ 1 low single bar	▬ 2 or 3 folded mats Plus,
▥ Landing mat or skill cushion	9 base mats (6 ft x 12 ft)
● gymnast	

Hand apparatus, balls, ropes, hoops, bean-bags, etc.

STATIONS

There are five stations in this circuit:

Single Bar—Position the bar about chest high over a single base mat or skill cushion.

Vault—Position two base mats end to end and center a vault on the mats. (For the vault, use a low horse, a mat shape [e.g., a trapezoid], a vaulting "box," or stacked bifold mats.) A vaulting board is also required. You may want to use a landing mat or skill cushion on the afterflight side of the vault.

Jump-Rope—Students perform manipulative skills in any open space, with or without mats.

Mat—Position two base mats end to end.

Balance—Surround a medium beam (about 3 feet high) with base mats for safety. Provide an additional landing mat or skill cushion because of the height of the beam.

Class organization 2 min.

Warm-up activities and games 4 min.

Explain the circuit 4 min.

1st rotation 4 min.

2nd rotation 4 min.

3rd rotation 4 min.

4th rotation 4 min.

5th rotation 4 min.

Warm-down and summary 5 min.

35 min total

STRENGTH DEVELOPMENT SKILLS

MAT
Inverted Balance

Press to headstand from prone position: This activity should be done with a spotter. From a prone position, with arms bent and the hands flat next to the shoulders (in the push-up position), the gymnast pushes the hips up by walking or sliding feet forward to a piked headstand, then straddles the legs, circling to the side and up to a stretched headstand held for 2 to 3 seconds.

Single leg swing up toward a handstand: From a front leaning support position, the gymnast lifts one leg up, leans forward on the arms, and switches leg positions, finishing by lowering the leg to the starting position.

3/4 Handstand, switching legs: From a straight standing position with the arms high, the gymnast lunges forward, lifting the back leg and placing the hands on the mat. Then the gymnast pushes off the front leg, extending up toward a handstand, switches leg positions, and lowers to a lunge, pushing off the hands and finishing in a straight stand.

VAULT
Squat Vaulting

Squat support, snap-down, squat support: From a squat support position on the mats, the gymnast extends the legs back and up, then quickly snaps the legs down, rebounding off the springboard and returning to a squat support.

Squat support, snap-down, squat support, straight jump: The gymnast repeats the action just described; on reaching the squat support, the gymnast immediately jumps up and forward to a straight body position, lands in a demi-plié, and extends the legs to a straight stand.

Rebounds, squat support, straight jump: From a stand on the springboard with hands on the mat, the gymnast rebounds 3 to 5 times, pulls the knees up to a squat support, immediately jumps up and forward to a straight body position, lands in a demi-plié, and extends the legs to a straight stand.

BALANCE
Mounting

Front leaning support mount: Facing the side of the beam, the gymnast places hands on top of the beam, pushes off the floor, and extends arms downward, finishing in front support (beam just below the hip).

Front support to straddle sit: The gymnast performs a front leaning support mount, then swings one leg sideward and up over the beam, turning the body to a straddle sit position on top of the beam, facing the end of the beam (Figure 8.12) with hands in front.

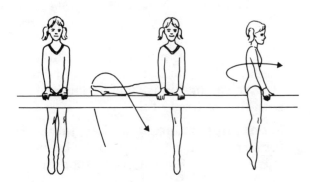

Figure 8.12 Gymnast performing a front support to a straddle sit.

Jump to one-foot squat support: Facing the side of the beam, the gymnast places hands on top of the beam, pushes off the floor, and extends arms downward while lifting one knee and placing the foot on the beam between the hands. The other leg remains straight and is extended against the side of the beam.

BAR
Hip Casting to Sole Circle

Jump to sole circle to stand: From a stand with arms extended and hands in overgrip, the gymnast jumps to a straddle

---

SAFETY TIPS

Use student assistants to enhance lesson goals and contribute to the safe conduct of activities. After proper instruction, they can be spotters for basic skills. Establish standard verbal cues to signal the beginning and end of activity sessions, and create orderly procedures for movement between stations.

---

position, with feet on the bar outside the hands. The gymnast must hold the feet on the bar through the lower vertical swing and then extend at the hip and release the grip, landing on both feet in front of the bar.

Jump to sole circle, underswing to stand: From a stand on folding mats, with arms extended and hands in overgrip, the gymnast jumps to a piked straddle position, placing feet on the bar through the lower vertical swing, and then directs the legs up away from the bar, extending at the hip. The gymnast should show flight after releasing the bar before landing on both feet in front of the bar.

Front support, stand on bar, jump off forward: This activity should be done with a spotter. From a front support posi-

---

TEACHING TIP

To allow more time for explanation and participation, you could reduce the number of stations in the circuit or reduce the number of skills at each station.

---

tion, the gymnast brings one foot up to the bar close to the hands, then moves either hand so that the foot is between the hands (you should hold either shoulder and wrist). Pushing up to standing position, the gymnast jumps forward off the bar, lands in a demi-plié, and extends the legs to a straight stand.

JUMP ROPE

Combinations

Figure 8/jump: The gymnast does a figure 8 (counterclockwise on the right side of the body, clockwise on the left), opens the rope to execute four single jumps with a forward turn of the rope, then immediately does another figure 8.

Figure 8/leap: The gymnast does a figure 8 (counterclockwise on the right side of the body, clockwise on the left), immediately opens the rope to execute a stride leap over a forward turn of the rope, then does another figure 8.

(Skills are performed with one end of the rope in each hand.)

Backward Circle Series

Saggital circles, clockwise: The gymnast circles the rope 5 times clockwise on the right side of the body.

Saggital circles, counterclockwise: The gymnast circles the rope 5 times counterclockwise on the left side of the body.

Figure 8: The gymnast alternates the counterclockwise and clockwise saggital circles, first to the right, then to the left.

(Skills are performed with one end of the rope in each hand.)

Lesson #4: *Coordination*

PACS SKILL OBJECTIVES

Psychomotor: To improve the coordination of gymnast's upper and lower body movements.

Affective: To foster feelings of positive self-image in the athletes using appropriate feedback and encouragement.

Cognitive: To develop gymnast's ability to relax before performing.

Social: To develop gymnast's etiquette in taking turns with space and equipment.

TIMETABLE

Lesson 4 adapts well to most gymnastics instructional settings. The variety of activities and the rotation times work in both physical education classes and gymnastics clubs.

FLOOR PLAN

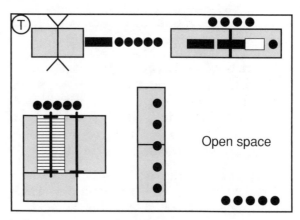

Equipment

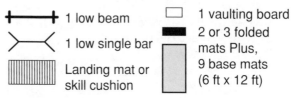

┼─────┼ 1 low beam

✕──✕ 1 low single bar

▥ Landing mat or skill cushion

☐ 1 vaulting board

▬ 2 or 3 folded mats Plus,

▨ 9 base mats (6 ft x 12 ft)

● gymnast

Hand apparatus, balls, ropes, hoops, bean-bags, etc.

STATIONS

There are five stations in this circuit:

Single Bar—Position the bar at chest height of the average size student over a single base mat or skill cushion. The gymnast should use a folded mat or mat shape (rectangle) to mount the bar.

Vault—Position two base mats end to end and center the vault on the mats. (For the vault, use a low horse, a mat shape [e.g., a trapezoid], a vaulting "box," or stacked bifold mats.) A vaulting board is also required. You may decide to use a landing mat or skill cushion on the afterflight side of the vault.

Jump Rope—Gymnasts may perform these skills in any open space, with or without mats.

Mat—Position two base mats end to end, then center a wedge mat on the base mats.

Balance—Surround a medium beam (about 3 feet high) with base mats for safety.

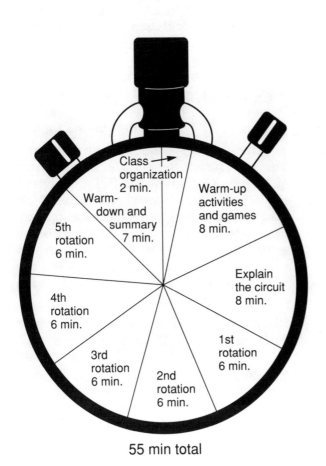

55 min total

COORDINATION SKILLS

MAT

Inverted Agility

Step-hurdle to cartwheel: The gymnast steps forward onto one foot, hurdles, and does a cartwheel, moving through a lunge and finishing facing the starting point.

Cartwheel-style roundoff: The gymnast performs a cartwheel and, as the first leg contacts the floor, quickly closes the second foot in beside the first, finishing in a straight standing position with arms high, facing toward the starting point.

Step into roundoff: The gymnast steps forward and raises one leg to perform a fast-paced cartwheel. Just before the first leg contacts the floor, both legs come together. In the finish, arms are high, knees are slightly flexed, and the gymnast faces the starting point.

VAULT

Jump Series

Traveling jumps over and back: Jumping leap frog style diagonally from one side of the mat to the other without landing on top of it, the gymnast travels forward after pushing off of both hands, raising the arms for each landing.

Squat to top of mat, forward roll: Standing on the springboard, the gymnast puts both hands on top of the mat, rebounds to a squat position on top of the mat, immediately executes a forward roll, and finishes in a standing position on top of the mat.

Vault to forward roll, jump, land, forward roll: The gymnast runs forward, rebounds off the board, and places hands on top of the mat to execute a forward roll. Upon finishing the roll, the gymnast performs a straight jump up and forward off the mat, landing on two feet, and finishes with a forward roll to a stand.

BALANCE

Dismounting

Jump off with 180° turn, land, 180° turn: Standing on the beam facing the end or side, the gymnast jumps forward and up off the beam, performs a 180° turn, lands on two feet, then jumps up, turning 180° and again landing on two feet, pausing momentarily in the landing position.

Front support to front dismount: From a front support on the beam, the gymnast flexes the knees and pushes up off the beam, then lowers the legs and lands on two feet on the mat, pausing momentarily in the landing position.

3/4 Handstand to stand: From a standing position, the gymnast lunges forward, places both hands on the beam, and lifts the back leg up, then pushes off the support foot, switches leg positions, pushes slightly to the side with the arms, brings both legs together, and lands on two feet.

BAR

Circling Forward

Single knee roll over forward: This activity should be done with a spotter. From a front support with hands in overgrip, the gymnast swings one leg sideward and up over the bar to a stride support, changing both hands to undergrip, then rolls forward (with a spot) to a single knee hang beneath the bar.

Single knee circle: This activity should be done with a spotter. From a front support with hands in overgrip, the gymnast swings one leg sideward and up over the bar to a stride support, changing both hands to undergrip, then shifts weight up and forward by pushing down with the arms. To complete the circle, the gymnast lifts the hips, hooks the front knee on the bar, leans forward, and swings back up to support (with a spot).

Stride circle (undergrip) with spot: This activity should be done with a spotter. From a front support with hands in overgrip, the gymnast swings one leg sideward and up over the bar to a stride support, changing both hands to undergrip, then extends the forward leg, shifts weight forward (with a spot), and circles the bar while maintaining the stride position with extended legs, finishing in a stride support (Figure 8.13).

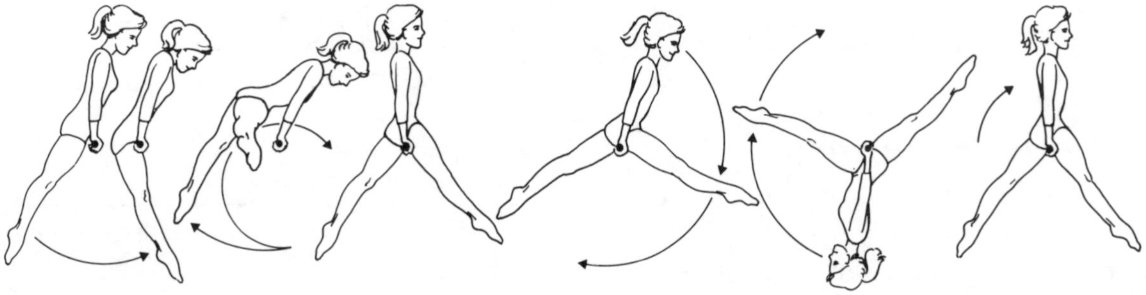

Figure 8.13   Gymnast performing a stride circle with an undergrip.

JUMP ROPE

Backward Circle Series

Saggital circles, clockwise: The gymnast circles the rope 5 times clockwise on the right side of the body.

Saggital circles, counteclockwise: The gymnast circles the rope 5 times counterclockwise on the left side of the body.

TEACHING TIPS

Plan rotation times to match your individual situation and objectives.

Because only one station (the single bar) requires spotting, you can generally supervise the group while assisting particular gymnasts at the single bar.

Figure 8: The gymnast alternates the counterclockwise and clockwise saggital circles, first to the right, then to the left.

(Skills are performed with both ends of the rope in the right hand, then repeated using the left hand.)

Combination

Figure 8/backward jump: The gymnast does a figure 8 (clockwise on the right side of the body, then counterclockwise on the left) and opens the rope to execute four single jumps over a backward turn of the rope, then immediately does another figure 8.

(Skill is performed with one end of the rope in each hand.)

Lesson #5: *Flexibility*

PACS SKILL OBJECTIVES

Psychomotor: To improve gymnast's flexibility for movements.

Affective: To create an atmosphere of respect for gymnastics skills, movements, apparatuses, and mats.

Cognitive: To develop gymnast's language skills, particularly the terms and phrases used to describe body movement.

Social: To help gymnasts be responsible for being prepared to participate in gymnastics class.

TIMETABLE

Lesson 5 works best with eight athletes. This instructional environment is more typical of gymnastics club programs, where several instructors may be working in the gym simultaneously and using multiple pieces of the same apparatuses.

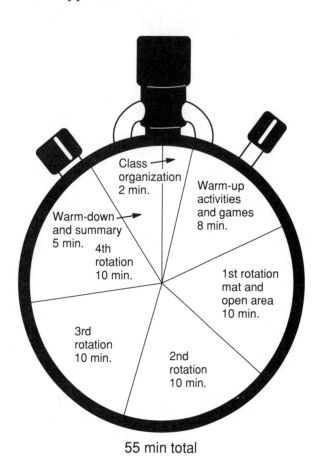

Class organization 2 min.

Warm-up activities and games 8 min.

Warm-down and summary 5 min.

4th rotation 10 min.

1st rotation mat and open area 10 min.

3rd rotation 10 min.

2nd rotation 10 min.

55 min total

FLOOR PLAN

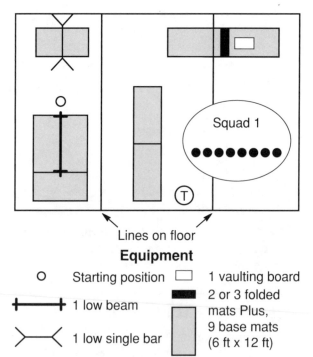

Lines on floor

Equipment

○   Starting position

┼   1 low beam

✕   1 low single bar

●   gymnast

☐   1 vaulting board

▬   2 or 3 folded mats Plus, 9 base mats (6 ft x 12 ft)

Hand apparatus, balls, ropes, hoops, bean-bags, etc.

Squad 1

T

STATIONS

There are four stations in this circuit:

Mat and Open Areas—This is a combined station. The tumbling strip is two base mats positioned end to end.

Balance—Surround a low beam with base mats for safety. Gymnasts can also use floor lines to practice locomotor skills.

Single Bar—Position the bar to a height that lets the taller athletes swing easily with bent knees. Place a single base mat or skill cushion under the bar.

Vault—Position two base mats end to end and center a vault on the mats. (For the vault, use a low horse, a mat shape [e.g., a trapezoid], a vaulting "box," or stacked bifold mats.) A vaulting horse is also required. You may want to use a landing mat or skill cushion on the afterflight side of the vault.

FLEXIBILITY SKILLS

MAT
Rolling Over Forward

Tip over from pike position: From a stretched standing position, the gymnast leans forward to place hands on the mat in front of the feet and continues by rolling forward, tucking as hips touch the mat and finishing in a straight standing position.

1/2 Handstand to forward roll: From a stretched standing position, the gymnast moves slowly through an arabesque, places hands on the floor, and executes a forward roll. The support leg remains in contact with the mat until the back touches the mat on the roll. The gymnast ends in a standing position (Figure 8.14).

Handstand forward roll: This activity should be done with a spotter. Passing through a handstand position, the gymnast lowers slowly to the upper back and completes a forward roll. Vary the skill by having the gymnast finish in different positions.

VAULT
Front Vaulting

Layout front vault: The gymnast rebounds off the board and vaults over the mats with the body extended, facing downward toward the mats and landing with the side of the body facing the mats.

Front vault, 90° turn to stand, facing mat: The gymnast rebounds off the board and vaults with the body extended, but as

> **TEACHING TIPS**
>
> To make better use of time in this lesson, you can break down the mat and open space station into another ''minicircuit'' or ''circuit within a circuit.'' Students can work at three stations simultaneously. This will keep the group active, giving them more opportunities to practice and have fun!
>
> Gymnasts can use a line painted on the floor near the balance station to practice locomotor skills.

Lesson #5

the body begins to descend the gymnast turns 90° toward the mat and lands facing the mat.

3/4 Cartwheel, 90° turn: Using several running steps, the gymnast rebounds off the springboard, extends the legs up and sideward through a 3/4 cartwheel position, then upon pushing off the hands turns 90° to face the mat. The gymnast pauses momentarily to show a good landing position.

BALANCE
Locomotor Activities

Stretch jump: Beginning with one foot in front of the other, the gymnast pushes off both feet to perform a stretch jump and lands on both feet on the beam.

Low leap: Beginning with one or two steps forward, the gymnast pushes off the

Figure 8.14   Gymnast performing a 1/2 handstand to a forward roll.

front foot and stretches the other forward to land.

Low tuck jump on beam: The gymnast pushes off the beam with both feet to execute a low tuck jump (without grasping the legs) and lands on both feet.

SAFETY TIP

Teach all balance beam skills on the floor before having the gymnasts move to successively higher beams.

BAR

Swinging

Swing through (piked and mixed grip), pivot on undergrip hand, stop, swing through (piked and overgrip): From a straight standing position with arms extended and hands on mixed grips, the gymnast swings under the bar in a pike position, stops momentarily, then executes a reverse pivot turn on the undergrip hand (both hands finish in overgrip). To finish, the gymnast swings back under the bar in pike position.

Swing through (tucked and overgrip), 180° turn, hesitate and release bar, single leg between arms to single leg hang: From a straight standing position with arms extended and hands in overgrip, the gymnast swings under the bar in a tuck position, hesitates, releases the bar, and turns 180°. The gymnast then regrips in overgrip, swings through, tapping off the floor, pulls one leg between the arms, and finishes in a single knee hang.

Swing through (tucked and overgrip), 180° turn, hesitate and release bar, swing through with a tap swing again to single knee up: From the single knee hang described in the previous skill, the gymnast swings again and executes a single knee up.

JUMP ROPE

Circle Series

Horizontal circles, overhead: The gymnast circles the rope 5 times overhead, keeping the rope horizontal.

Horizontal circles, over and under: The gymnast circles the rope twice overhead, keeping the rope horizontal, then immediately swings the rope low to horizontal circles, jumps over the rope twice, then moves the rope back up to horizontal circles overhead.

(Skills are performed with both ends of the rope in the right hand, then repeated using the left hand. Skills are also performed both clockwise and counterclockwise.)

Combinations

Figure 8/run: With one end of the rope in each hand, the gymnast does a figure 8 (counterclockwise circle to the left, counterclockwise to the right). Then, while performing continuous figure 8s, the gymnast runs forward, completing each figure 8 in three running steps.

Figure 8/run, right hand: With both ends of the rope in the right hand, the gymnast does a figure 8 (clockwise to the left, counterclockwise to the right) and then a forward run, completing each figure 8 in three steps.

Figure 8/run, left hand: With both ends of the rope in the left hand, the gymnast does a figure 8 (counterclockwise to the right, clockwise to the left) and then a forward run, completing each figure 8 in three steps.

Lesson #6: *Muscular Endurance*

PACS SKILL OBJECTIVES

Psychomotor: To develop gymnast's muscular endurance by using repetitive anaerobic movements.

Affective: To teach gymnast to take responsibility for actions.

Cognitive: To enhance gymnast's concentration by using verbal and visual cues during skill performance.

Social: To develop gymnasts' respect for equipment and apparatuses as they help move equipment around the gym.

TIMETABLE

In this lesson, you are responsible for one squad of eight students. Rotate the athletes to each station. The lesson devotes most of the time to warm-up, mat, and open areas to assist in meeting the lesson's objectives.

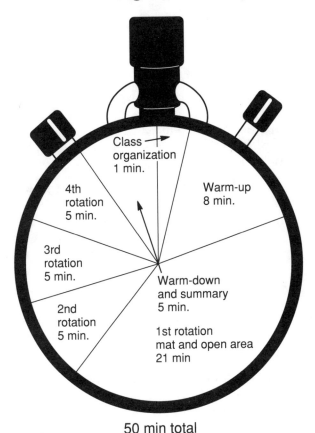

Class organization 1 min.

Warm-up 8 min.

4th rotation 5 min.

3rd rotation 5 min.

2nd rotation 5 min.

Warm-down and summary 5 min.

1st rotation mat and open area 21 min

50 min total

FLOOR PLAN

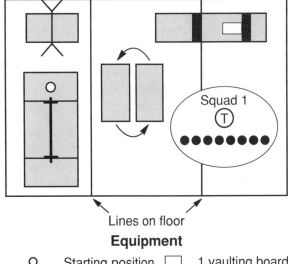

Squad 1

Lines on floor

Equipment

○   Starting position

◻   1 vaulting board

╪   1 low beam

⬛   2 or 3 folded mats Plus,

⟩⟨   1 low single bar

▨   9 base mats (6 ft x 12 ft)

●   gymnast

Hand apparatus, balls, ropes, hoops, bean-bags, etc.

STATIONS

There are four stations in this circuit:

Mat and Open Areas—This is a combined station. The tumbling strip is two base mats positioned next to each other so gymnasts can perform up one mat and down the other.

Balance—Surround a low beam with base mats for safety.

Single Bar—Position the bar chest high over a single base mat or skill cushion.

Vault—Position two base mats end to end and use two folded panel mats as vaulting stations, one with a vaulting board and one without.

MUSCULAR ENDURANCE SKILLS

Lesson
#6

MAT
Roll Over Backward

Roll backward to momentary shoulder balance: The gymnast rolls backward from a sitting position to a balance position on the upper back and shoulders. With arms extended overhead, once in balance the gymnast should demonstrate the stretch, straddle, tuck, and pike positions.

Backward roll from straddle stand: The gymnast rolls backward from a straddle stand and finishes in a squat stand.

Straddle backward roll: The gymnast starts in a straddle position, either standing or sitting, rolls backward, pushes off the hands, and finishes in a straddle stand.

VAULT
Flank and Rear Vaulting

One leg vault on and over panel mats without board: Walking up to the panel mats, the gymnast hops onto the mats, supports self with one hand and one foot (fingers of the support hand pointing toward the long end of the mats), then hops off the other side of the mats to land standing with side facing the mats.

Vault one foot on top, and over, land back to mats: The gymnast rebounds off the springboard to a support position on one hand and one foot on top of the mats, then immediately pushes off and over the mats to a two-foot landing with back toward the mats.

Modified flank vault (one leg tucked): The gymnast rebounds off the springboard to a support position on top of the mat (both hands), then, as the legs move sideward, shifts weight to the opposite side of the movement. With one leg tucked and the other extended, the body passes over the mats and the gymnast lands with back toward the mats.

BALANCE
Dismounting

Step off end: From a standing position on the beam, the gymnast steps forward off the beam to a two-foot landing, showing a demi-plié before straightening the legs to a stand.

Stretch jump off beam: From a standing position on the beam, the gymnast jumps up and forward off the end or side of the beam, shows a stretched position, and lands on two feet.

Tuck jump off beam: From a standing position on the end or side of the beam, the gymnast executes a tuck jump and lands on two feet on the mat.

SAFETY TIP

Spotting includes observation as well as hands-on assistance with skills. Although none of the listed skills specifically includes spotting, you should closely observe each performance and "be ready" should any mishap occur.

BAR
Circling Backward

Step, lift leg, pull to bar: From a stand, the gymnast steps forward under the bar, lifts the back leg forward and up, pulls the hip up to the bar, then slowly lowers the body back to the floor.

Stretch hip pullover (single leg push-off from folded mat): From a stand with hands in overgrip, the gymnast steps forward and pushes off the folded mat with one leg while lifting the other leg up and over the bar (folded mat should be placed below or slightly in front of the bar). Simultaneously the gymnast pulls the bar toward the hips, brings legs together over the bar, and rotates shoulders backward to a front support (Figure 8.15).

Back hip pullover (single leg push with bar chest high): From a stand, the gymnast steps forward under the bar, lifts the back leg forward and up, pulls the hip up to the bar, rotates the shoulders backward, and finishes in a front support.

Figure 8.15 Gymnast performing a stretch hip pullover.

JUMP ROPE

Run and Jump

Run and jump: Beginning with the left foot, the gymnast runs forward three steps while executing a saggital figure 8, starting on the left side with clockwise circles, then opens the ropes, jumps four times over a forward turn of the rope, and immediately repeats the exercise.

Run and leap: Beginning with the left foot, the gymnast runs forward three steps while executing a saggital figure 8, starting on the left side of the body with clockwise circles, opens the rope and leaps with the right foot over a forward turn of the rope, and immediately repeats the exercise.

(Skills are performed with students traveling across the floor in lines, holding one end of the rope in each hand. Do a mirror image repeat for each skill.)

TEACHING TIPS

With so much time devoted to one station, make sure gymnasts understand the expectations for behavior. Remember that this is one of the objectives of the lesson.

As the gymnasts wait in line for their turn, encourage them to pay attention, observing the performance of others to help their learning.

Writers and Contributors

Michael P. Jackie, USGF Executive Director, Indianapolis, Indiana; *Stephen W. Whitlock,* USGF Director of Educational Services and Safety, Indianapolis, Indiana; *David Moskovitz,* Executive Editor, USGF Coaching Development Coordinator, Indianapolis, Indiana; *William A. Sands,* PhD, Chair, USGF Sport Science Advisory Committee, University of Utah; *Gerald S. George,* PhD, University of Southwest Louisiana; *Patty Hacker,* PhD, Chair, USGF Educational Subcommittee, South Dakota State University; *James Nance,* University of Kentucky at Lexington; *Nora Hitzel,* USGF Rhythmic Program Administrator, Indianapolis, Indiana; *Terry Exner,* GymMarin, San Rafael, California; *Eric Malmberg,* State University College at Cortland, New York; *Alan Tilove,* Spectrum Juggling, Seattle, Washington; *Susan True,* National Federation of State High School Associations, Kansas City, Missouri; *James H. Stephenson,* University of Utah.

Gymnastics and Coaching Books

(Updated Second Edition)

Rainer Martens

1997 ▪ Paper ▪ 232 pp
Item PMAR0666
ISBN 0-88011-666-8
$18.95 ($27.95 Canadian)

The revised edition of this popular book provides updated information and useful advice for coaches of all sports at the high school or club level and above. You'll find valuable information on developing a positive coaching philosophy, applying the principles of sport psychology and sport physiology to your coaching, teaching sport skills properly, and using sport management skills effectively. The book is filled with self-evaluation tests, summaries, and illustrations.

Rae Pica

1988 ▪ Cloth ▪ 160 pp
Item PPIC0306
ISBN 0-88011-306-5
$25.00 ($37.50 Canadian)

In **Dance Training for Gymnastics**, Rae Pica tells how dance trainers can help gymnasts of all ages and skill levels improve overall performance, reduce the chance of injury, and develop a distinctive style.

The text clearly explains how to implement specific steps from ballet, jazz, modern dance, and movement education in floor exercises and balance beam performances. Pica also offers guidelines for choosing an instructor, selecting music, choreographing routines, and more.

Denise A. Gula

1990 ▪ Paper ▪ 176 pp
Item PGUL0364
ISBN 0-88011-364-2
$19.95 ($26.95 Canadian)

Dance Choreography for Competitive Gymnastics focuses exclusively on how dance techniques can—and should—be applied to the training of gymnasts. While other texts offer only isolated examples of individual dance steps that might be used by gymnasts, this book helps the reader use combinations of dance steps to create complete choreographed sequences for floor and beam routines.

The book also includes 38 ready-to-use routines from a wide variety of dance movement styles.

ASEP Volunteer Level

The American Sport Education Program (ASEP) offers three Volunteer Level curriculums for adults who work with youth sport: SportCoach, SportParent, and SportDirector. The SportCoach Program consists of two courses. The **Rookie Coaches Course** provides inexperienced coaches with essential information for teaching the skills and strategies of a sport, including sample practice plans. The **Coaching Young Athletes Course** is for second-year coaches and others who want more instruction in the principles of coaching than is offered in the Rookie Course.

ASEP's SportParent Course is a 1- to 2-hour program that provides youth sport administrators and coaches with a practical and effective way to educate parents about their children's participation in sports.

ASEP's SportDirector program offers outstanding opportunities for youth sport directors to improve sport programs for the children in their community. The program includes a very practical *Youth SportDirector Guide* and a dynamic workshop.

Call **Toll-Free 1-800-747-5698** for more information on ASEP.

Place your credit card order today! (VISA, AMEX, MC)
TOLL FREE: U.S. (800) 747-4457 ▪ Canada (800) 465-7301
OR: U.S. (217) 351-5076 ▪ Canada (519) 971-9500
FAX: U.S. (217) 351-2674 ▪ Canada (519) 971-9797

Human Kinetics
http://www.humankinetics.com/
The Premier Publisher for Sports & Fitness